STRAIGHTFORWARD

GUIDE TO

BUYING, SELLING AND MAKING A HEALTHY PROFIT FROM ONLINE TRADING SITES

Paul Welwyn

Straightforward Publishing
www.straightforwardco.co.uk

Straightforward Guides

ISBN
978-1-84716-455-1

Printed by Grosvenor Group Ltd London

Cover design by Straightforward Graphics

CONTENTS

Introduction

PART 2. SETTING UP ON YOUR OWN

Introduction to This Book

E Commerce opportunities

This book is about how to profit from buying and selling goods on online auction/trading sites. Indeed, how to make a decent living by using these sites. In addition to describing the various sites, the book details a step-by-step guide to registering and selling plus offering invaluable tips on business management.

Traditionally, the platform for selling goods to other people has been (is) the shop or the market or other venues such as boot sales, mail order and so on. Ecommerce has become a major new entrant into the world of selling. However, instead of a bricks and mortar shop you now have a virtual shop, created online. This is what this book is all about-selling online and making a profit doing so.

Ecommerce consists of everything that is sold online. And masses of goods are sold on line. Essentially we have been through a retail revolution and this is evolving all the time. Two main players have developed, eBay and Amazon and they are massive. eBay has over 17 million visitors each month in the UK and over 200 million globally, operating in more than 40 countries. Amazon too is massive. Each site differs slightly and these difference are brought out in the book.

The main point underlying everything is that, once you have created your selling platform, you need always to bear in mind that you are like every other business, you need to keep costs under control, price your products, present them well, offer good customer service, and expand and grow.

Although I will deal mainly with eBay and Amazon, the two giants, and detail how they operate and how to use them effectively, there are also a number of other prominent smaller sites that I will mention. Once we have covered the main sites thoroughly, then the same principles can be used when exploring these other smaller sites.

In addition, there is a section which covers setting up your own online business, separate from the big players, although if you go down this route you can also integrate and sell your products through eBay and Amazon and any other smaller site that you choose.

This book is aimed at those who aspire to create a profitable business on the main auction sites, and smaller sites, and is also aimed at those who might wish to develop their own web store independently of the big players.

We start off with eBay and a history of eBay and how it achieved its massive status, explaining what eBay is and what it isn't.

Good luck with your venture!

****

Chapter 1

All About eBay

A Short History of eBay

eBay was founded in Pierre Omidyar's San Jose living room back in September 1995. It was, from the start, meant to be a marketplace for the sale of goods and services for individuals.

In 1998, Pierre and his co-founder Jeff Skoll brought in Meg hitman to sustain the success. Meg had studied at the Harvard

Business School and had learned the importance of branding at companies such as Hasbro (an American toy manufacturer).

Meg culled her senior staff from companies such as Pepsico and Disney, created an experienced management team with an average of 20 years of business experience and built a strong vision for the company -- that eBay is a company that's in the business of **connecting people**, not selling them things. It is when people are connected that they buy and sell.

The Business Model

eBay has built an online person-to-person trading community on the Internet, using the World Wide Web. Buyers and sellers are brought together in a manner where sellers are permitted to list items for sale, buyers to bid on items of interest and all eBay users to browse through listed items in a fully automated way. The items are arranged by topics, where each type of auction has its own category.

eBay has both streamlined and globalized person-to-person trading, (which has traditionally been conducted through such forms as market sales, collectibles shows, flea markets and more), with their web interface. This facilitates easy exploration for buyers and enables the sellers to immediately list an item for sale within minutes of registering.

Though the first things sold on eBay were collectibles and home items, the company branched out to higher profile sellers like Disney and General Motors. These companies sell items in the same manner as the individual sellers. The eBay community was resistant to these changes at first but soon grew accustomed to the presence of big business hosting auctions.

The Website Half.com was bought by eBay in 2000 and fully integrated into eBay's web community in 2001. Half.com allows users to buy and sell items at lower rates much like eBay but without the auction feature. In October of 2002 eBay acquired Paypal Inc. for $1.5 billion. Paypal is the preferred way of making payments for eBay auctions and is growing in popularity for other Internet uses. Paypal allows a person to send or receive money via an email address. Money in a Paypal account can be spent on the Internet, sent by check to the account owner, or deposited into a bank account. Paypal also offers credit cards, debit cards, and a bill paying function.

What is eBay?

Having looked at the history of the development of eBay, we can look specifically at what the purpose of the site is.

- **A place to buy.** Get nearly anything you need or want at prices better than you can find in traditional bricks-and-mortar or even online stores. Though there are lots of bad deals on eBay too, the careful consumer can always come out ahead. Vey soon, it will now be possible, for example, to buy paintings and other fine art from Sotheby's. So, if you fancy a Picasso or Warhol you can get one on eBay.

- **A place to sell.** Whether you're a big retailer or just an average Joe cleaning out your house or garage, nearly anything you list on eBay *will sell* if you're flexible enough about the price. eBay's global reach can even move unusual items that aren't in demand in your own area.

- **A meeting place, not a store.** eBay doesn't actually sell any goods itself. All of the goods on eBay are sold and delivered by third party sellers that are neither employed by, nor have any other relationship with, eBay itself.

Instead, eBay's business is to give entrepreneurs and sellers a place to reach buyers, and to give buyers access to the world's largest collection of things for sale. As we said above, eBay connects people.

- **A place to shop.** Because of the immense variety of things that can be found for sale on eBay, many members have discovered that eBay is one of the best places in the world to window or comparison shop. The millions of item listings created by sellers often include photos, detailed descriptions, and owner experiences (very important for a seller, as we shall see). Because you can see lots of the same item side-by-side in various conditions and know what each one sold or is selling for, eBay gives you insight into the real market value or "street value" of most types of goods around the world.

- **A place to collect.** eBay is the world's largest marketplace for rare, discontinued, collectible, or hard-to-find items, no matter what the type or price. Whether you're looking for turn-of-the-century box cameras, hand-made Victorian doilies, Soviet army service medals, or 1980s vintage arcade games, eBay will give you a better selection than just about anyone else anywhere.

- **A website.** There is no physical eBay store. Founded in San Jose but now operated from several cities, eBay's service exists entirely online, and all aspects of business other than the delivery of bought and sold items themselves are typically handled through the eBay website.

- **Free for buyers and inexpensive for sellers.** It costs nothing to become an eBay member, to shop for goods, or to purchase goods from eBay sellers. Sellers pay a minimal amount to list items for sale, and another small

14

percentage of the value when an item is sold. There are no monthly fees or other hidden costs.

- **Like the real world in many ways.** Just as you'll encounter both honest and dishonest people in the real world, you'll find both honest people and crooks on eBay. Thankfully, eBay's site includes a selection of tools like the feedback system that are designed to help you to remain safe as an eBay member.

eBay is now a marketplace where individuals and business sell to an online audience of about 17 million people a month in the United Kingdom. As it is global in scope eBay also helps people and business buy and sell with people all over the world.

In a nutshell

Sellers offer goods for sale using an online form to post a written description of their wares and also post a picture of the goods. Buyers can either bid using an online auction system or buy instantly using the Buy It Now feature (more about that later). Buyers judge the trustworthiness of sellers using a feedback system of user reviews. Some eBay sellers are accredited as Top-Rated sellers for delivering consistent good service.

As stated above, eBay acquired Paypal as a payment service and almost universally buyers and sellers on eBay will use this service. Sellers sometimes offer free postage and packing to buyers, but if there are carriage costs involved these will usually be covered by the buyer. Postage costs are detailed on the View Item particulars when the buyer examines the item.

Once payment is received by the sellers, the item will be despatched. As mentioned, sellers pay listing fees to place their items for sale on eBay and also pay a Final Value Fee commission on a successful sale. The fee and commission depends on the value of the goods sold and also the category that they were listed in. Both buyer and seller can then leave feedback for their trading partner depending on how it all went.

In the event of things going wrong, which they can sometimes do, buyers are covered by eBay Buyer Protection and sellers who get ripped off by a buyer are also protected by eBay. Although there are processes in place to stop fraud, like any other form of trading the potential is always there.

In the next chapter, we will look at the process of registering on eBay. However, before registration, it is necessary to look at the basic equipment that you will need to function as a trader.

A good computer

This is the most important piece of kit that you will need. No computer, no eBay! The computer you have will need access to the web, the faster the better. Whether you use Apple or PC is neither here nor there although some of eBays features are not compatible with Apple mac. However, there are ways to get round this so you can use a Mac or PC.

Digital images

I mentioned above that you will need to post a photo with a description of your goods. You can use a digital camera or a smartphone to take these. If you are using a smartphone this will need to be combined with an eBay mobile app.

As more and more customers are buying using their mobile phones then it is very important that crystal clear imagery is used. If you post up a poor image then it is very likely that a potential buyer will move on. Remember, as a trader you will be competing with other traders selling the same type of good.

A flatbed scanner as well as a digital camera will be useful, particularly if you are selling small items or paper items that will fit on the screen, such as stamps or postcards or jewellery.

Printing and packing

You will need a good quality printer because you will have to print out despatch notes and other paperwork. If you intend to trade for a profit on eBay think of yourself as a business person and make sure you are well equipped from the outset. My advice would be to use a laser printer as they are more efficient and faster than ink jet, and also cheaper to run. It's also a good idea to ensure that you have a supply of good quality packing material, padded envelopes, bubble wrap and cardboard. As a trader, think quality and think safety and make sure you use decent packaging.

The use of mobiles in e-commerce

The buzzword here is M-Commerce or mobile commerce. As many people now access the web using a smartphone, so an increasing amount of trading is carried out via mobile phone or tablets such as iPads. This has transformed how people buy and sell on eBay as they can do this on the move.

If you want to join this ever-growing army of people, you will need to get the relevant apps for your devices. On many phones nowadays, such apps will be pre-loaded or you can get them via the app store for your gadget. The full array of eBay apps can be accessed at:
https://anywhere.ebay.co.uk/mobile/iphone/ebay/

You can also get apps for PayPal or Amazon and all sorts of other e commerce sites. You will need such apps not only to use for your own purchasing, but to see what your listings look like on a mobile device. If they look good then fine. However, if they look grainy or unclear you will have to do some work to smarten up your images.

In the next chapter, we will look at how to register on eBay so that you can begin your journey to becoming a successful trader.

****

Chapter 2

Using eBay-Initial Steps to Register

Registering on eBay

Actually registering with eBay is a simple process. The very first step is to go to the main eBay site and provide your personal details as in the below example.

Get Started on eBay

See form overleaf.
Create your personal account or start a business account.

First name

Surname

Email

Create your password

Confirm password

By clicking 'Submit' I agree that:
- I accept the User Agreement.
- I give consent to the processing of my data- .
- I may receive communications from eBay and I understand that I can change my notification preferences at any time in My eBay.
- I am at least 18 years old.

As you can see, the first step is to provide your personal and contact details, i.e. your name and address and your contact number. Because eBay is so hot on fraud, it is very important indeed that you put in the correct details. If the information that you enter is false you will be suspended from eBay with immediate effect. You will then be asked to provide proof of identity, which is time consuming and gets you off to a bad start.

Because eBay communicates with its members by email it is obviously vital that you give them an email address that you have regular access to. You will need to type the address in twice to confirm that it is correct. You then have to choose your user ID and password. You should take time to think about your User ID as it is important and easy to forget. So, obviously, create a User ID that you can remember. The same goes with your password. Make sure that your User ID is sensible as a stupid sounding one may put off other traders.

When all the sections on the form have been completed and you have pressed the 'submit' button you will be taken to the next page where you will be asked to accept and agree to eBay's user agreement and privacy policy. If you actually want to read it, you can print it out. Once you are satisfied and click to accept, eBay will send you an email, which is their way of checking that the email is correct. When you receive the email, click the 'confirm registration' button inside. That will take you to eBay and you are then a fully registered member, ready to use the site.

If you choose to use an email address that is not personalised, i.e. outlook or yahoo, then be prepared to have to provide credit or debit card details. This is a way for eBay to ensure safety and protect people who use the site.

The email from eBay may take up to 24 hours to arrive so don't worry, sit tight. If it doesn't arrive then you can request that it is sent again. You can do this via the 'confirm registration' link on the site.

In Chapter 3 we will look at the process of buying goods on eBay. **You will need to put yourself in the shoes of a buyer**, especially if you are becoming a trader, with the goal of making a living off the site.

****

Chapter 3

Buying Goods on eBay

Having covered the initial basics of eBay and how to register, it is now time to look at buying goods on eBay. To be a successful seller you need to walk through the process in the shoes of a buyer. This will enable you to see how other sellers present goods, the quality of their shop windows and also to look at costing and postage.

As we mentioned, eBay is not really about auctions. Sure, you can put in bids for goods, and that is how the company started. However, nowadays the actual process of bidding for goods is really only a small part of the activities of eBay. eBay is mainly a marketplace where new items are sold alongside used items. People use the BUY IT NOW (BIN) system and a great deal of what is sold is sold by big retailers. However, many other people are involved and it's important to understand what the site is about before you focus on what it is you want to sell. You should do this by registering and cruising the site to get a feel of what is available.

The importance of listing

One thing that you will notice when you cruise the site is the importance of listing in the advertising process. You should make a note of the way things are listed as this will be important to you as a seller. There are many listings on the site that are accompanied by very potent ads, photos, descriptions etc., and you should begin to note all of the less than effective ads, such as those with shoddy photos, inadequate or overblown text etc. As a seller, you will be aiming at the perfect advertisement that will cause people to buy from you.

One thing to watch out for, at the outset, is that a lot of eBay specific terms and acronyms are used across the site. If you get confused you can access a glossary developed by eBay at https://pages.eBay.co.uk/help/glossary.html as well as a guide to acronyms in its help section:

http://pages.ebay.co.uk/help/account/acronyms.html

User feedback on eBay

As with all good sites, eBay has developed a feedback system which helps buyers rate sellers. Every eBay member has a Feedback Profile, which includes basic information about the member and the Feedback that their trading partners have left for them. Learning to trust a member is influenced by what their past buyers or sellers have to say.

For each transaction, the buyer and seller can rate each other by leaving Feedback.

A buyer can leave positive, neutral or negative Feedback along with a comment. The buyer can also rate the seller on additional criteria such as accuracy of item description, communication, dispatch time and postage and packaging charges. **These detailed seller ratings** do not count toward the Feedback Score and are anonymous. This means that sellers can't tell which buyer left which detailed rating, so buyers can feel free to leave ratings that honestly tell the story about their experience.

If a seller wants to leave Feedback for a buyer, they can leave positive Feedback and a short comment.

Leaving honest comments about a particular eBay member gives other Community members a good idea of what to expect when dealing with that member. Once it's left, Feedback becomes a permanent part of the member's Feedback Profile.

Buyers can leave Feedback for a seller after a transaction ends. But if they are leaving Feedback for a specific seller again, that repeat Feedback will not be calculated in the seller's Feedback Score unless the repeat transaction occurred in a separate week.

With this Feedback approach, buyers can reward their favourite sellers not only with sales but also with helping spread the word about the seller's services. And sellers can return the favour by leaving similar Feedback for favourite buyers once a week.

Buyers rate sellers from 1-5 stars and once you have been through the process it becomes second nature. eBay also lists top-rated sellers who have consistently received excellent feedback.

The importance of getting postage costs right

If you look at eBay, you will see that there are many weird and wonderful Postage costs. If, as a seller, you don't get this element right you will lose a sale. If at all possible, a bonus point is to include postage and packing in the sale cost. However, if you can't do this for economic reasons you should try to get the postage costs as accurate as possible, don't guess or levy a high cost.

In addition to postage, you should realise that buyers like to get an item on time. If you buy a good from Amazon, you can get next day service. likewise with many other sites. If you become a seller make sure that you have your delivery times sorted. Do this and buyers will come back.

How to trade safely on eBay

A lot of people have their doubts about eBay and stories are legion about people getting ripped off.

Below is one recent example of a person trading on eBay who had the express intention of ripping customers off. He was banned from eBay for life.

An artist who sold imitation paintings on eBay, allegedly passing them off as genuine works by artists such as LS Lowry and Adrian Heath, had been selling about three paintings a week from his flat claiming to have found many of them in his father's collection or at art fairs. In many cases, the artist, would allegedly place the paintings for sale on eBay and inform potential bidders that the paintings were "signed", suggesting that they had been signed by the artist.

The listings would then claim that there was no paperwork available to prove that they were genuine, offering to sell them as "after the artist", a term used to describe work made as a copy or in the same style as a major artist.

This explained how the listings were seemingly able to offer LS Lowry paintings for just £360, when real Lowry works have sold for over £1 million. It is believed that the artist painted many of the imitation works himself.

On the auction page for one Lowry painting, the listing said "Churchyard scene, signed oil painting in guilt [sic] wooden frame .... This belonged to my father ... I have no paperwork or history and sell it as 'after-Lowry'".

One eBay listing offered a work by Adrian Heath, the leading British abstract artist. The listing said: "Superb abstract oil painting on board signed." It added: "Lacking paperwork - selling as manner of artist."

However, problems began when the man reportedly sold one of his paintings to an undercover reporter posing as an eBay customer. The Sunday Telegraph reported yesterday that he was arrested and cautioned for "fraud by false representation". The fraud reportedly involved an imitation of a work by Ashley Jackson, a living artist whose watercolours can sell for up to £40,000. A listing on eBay offered a "genuine Ashley Jackson original watercolour signed 1972." Mr Jackson complained to his local fraud squad and told The Sunday Telegraph: "These forgeries have a terrible effect on my reputation."

A spokesman for eBay said that the man had been banned for life because he had not "lived up to the high standards we expect." The spokesman added: "Sellers may not disclaim knowledge of or responsibility for, the authenticity or legality of the items they offer in their listings."

As a seller, you will need to understand the buyers fears when purchasing on eBay. The main problems are not receiving goods or receiving shoddy goods or receiving fake goods, as in the above example. In Chapter 7, I will outline the legal rights of the buyer and also eBay's system of redress.

Here are a number of essential tips that the buyer should heed when purchasing on eBay:

- **Always contact the seller before a bid.** This helps the buyer get a good idea of what kind of a seller they are. This also allows them to ask questions about the object. They don't always include every detail. Whether it is a mistake or not, the listings should be very accurate, so if there's any question about what something includes or doesn't, if it has a return policy or not, or anything they might not understand, you should email the seller. If they do not email you back, do not bid on the item unless your question wasn't going to affect your bidding. If anything should go wrong, and you have a good explanation, you can retract your bid if it's before the auction ends.

- **Read the description very carefully.** If you made a mistake, misread, didn't read the whole description, etc., you can't blame the seller. If you buy an item that you don't want because you made a mistake, it's yours. The only way to send it back is if the seller has a returns policy. Then again, you could refuse to accept it, but you would have to deal with eBay. If the description isn't clear, don't bid on it. Email the seller and ask in detail about what you don't understand.

- **Take a look at the seller's feedback.** If they have good feedback, you can probably trust them. Also, look at some of the comments they've received. Sometimes a seller will get pretty bad comments. Depending on what the comment is about, you can probably determine whether you should bid on the item. Also, look at the type of items the seller usually sells. If the item you're looking at is unlike anything they usually sell, it could be cause for suspicion.

- **Make sure you know how they would make you pay.** Some sellers use PayPal, which is very helpful when it comes time to pay. If they want your credit card number and you don't want to give it to them, use an alternative way to pay. If there are no other alternative ways, you will have to give them your card number, although most sellers use PayPal or another type of payment system.

- **Always total up the cost of the item and the postage cost, and the insurance cost should you choose to put insurance on it.** Sometimes the item will sell for a pretty low price, until you look at the postage cost. You could end up paying much, much more than you had planned because you didn't look at the postage cost.

- **Make sure you know how long it will take for the item to get to you.** If the item is for a birthday, Christmas, or any other type of present, make sure that the item will reach you within enough time. In reality, you can't find out what day, hour, minute, or second it will arrive, but you should get an approximation. If it doesn't reach you in the approximated time, contact the seller. Do not contact eBay. It might not have arrived when you expected for a number of reasons: the seller didn't send it soon enough, there were problems with the mail, etc. If the seller sent it, then it's neither your nor the seller's fault. The seller should then contact the mail service. If the problem is with the seller, such as he changed his mind and doesn't want to sell, then contact eBay. They will take care of the matter. You might not get your item but you will get your money back, and most likely the seller will be banned from eBay for a while.

- **Always note the item number.** This is the best way to keep track of an item you have won, bid on, or are planning to bid on. Sometimes the auction will be taken off of eBay for certain reasons. If you need to email the seller about an item not arriving to you, and the auction has been removed from eBay because it's over, you can type in the item number and get all the information you need from the auction page.

- **Check if a return policy is offered.** Sellers that stand behind their products will offer a return policy. Be sure to read the terms and conditions as most return policies expire very quickly.

In chapter 7, we explore the legal rights of buyers on sites such as eBay.

* * * * * * * * * * * * * *

Chapter 4

Selling Goods on eBay-The First Practical Steps to Take

Create a Seller's Account

Before you can start to sell, you need to attend to the preliminaries, in much the same way that you did as a buyer. Before you can sell your first item you need to create a Seller's Account. This is quite simple but you need to get it right. You fill in an online form and provide information that will act as a verification process. The first step is to click 'sell' in the navigation bar on the eBay.co.uk homepage then on the Sell Hub you need to click 'Sell my Item' and sign in again.

When you create your seller's account you will need a credit or debit card, You will also need the postal address relating to the card. eBay will ask you to verify your personal details and how you wish to pay your ebay fees. Although you can choose the credit or debit card you have entered, PayPal is usually the easiest and preferred option.

Registering a business on eBay

As we mentioned in the previous chapter, many businesses register on eBay. Huge concerns such as Argos trade regularly. However, the vast majority are small to medium size businesses. There is a different procedure for business registration. If you are a business, you must let the site know this. The Selling Regulations require that you give information such as registered address and VAT number (if relevant), so that this is available to buyers. If you need to register as a business you should visit http://pages.ebay.co.uk/services/registration/businesslanding.ht ml.

On this page, there is legal guidance for business sellers. You will also need to register on PayPal as a business user. There are a lot of perks available on PayPal, not least discounted fees for volume sales. If you are accepting more than £1500 a month in payments, you can get this reduction. You will need to apply as you wont get it automatically. To register, log into PayPal and click the merchant services link on your account page.

eBay's selling policies

Knowing the rules and policies on eBay can help you become a more successful seller. So before listing your item, make sure you read, understand, and regularly check their policies (including the rules for sellers and the eBay User Agreement and all applicable laws and regulations on the sale of your item. This can help you avoid potential problems.

eBay's policies are intended to:

- Support laws and regulations
- Minimise risks to sellers
- Provide equal opportunity to all sellers
- Protect intellectual property rights
- Provide an enjoyable buying experience
- Support the values of the eBay Community

Make sure your listing follows their guidelines. If it doesn't, it may be removed, and your buying and selling privileges could be limited.

Prohibited and restricted items

eBay's policies are often based on country laws, although in some cases, they may also be based on input from their customers and their own discretion, especially for dangerous or sensitive items.

eBay policies cover 3 main areas – prohibited, restricted, and potentially infringing items.

Prohibited items are not allowed to be sold on eBay, often because they're illegal or involve strict federal or state regulations. Examples include:

- o Chance listings that promote giveaways, random drawings, raffles, or prizes
- o Firearms, weapons, and knives

- o Offensive material, which includes items that are racially or ethnically inappropriate
  - o Prohibited services, which include services that are illegal or sexual in nature or that violate the eBay User Agreement
- Restricted items can generally be sold on eBay but only under certain conditions that sellers are required to meet. Examples of items include:
  - o Artefacts and grave-related items
  - o Food and healthcare items
- Potentially infringing items may be in violation of certain copyrights, trademarks, or other intellectual property rights. So some items aren't allowed (even though they may be legal) because they often violate copyright or trademark laws. This also applies to certain types of information that appear in listings. Here are some examples:
  - o Replicas, counterfeit items, and unauthorised copies
  - o Sellers can't deny or reject any knowledge of or responsibility for the authenticity or legality their items (see our authenticity disclaimer policy).
  - o You're not allowed to use other members' pictures or text (see images and text policy).

To avoid creating listings that infringe upon intellectual property rights, read how eBay protects intellectual property. You can also take their intellectual property tutorial.

And remember: offering a prohibited, restricted, or potentially infringing item for free (rather than for sale) protects you from potential liability. This policy applies to both sellers and buyers.

Listing practices

As a general rule, sellers have to:

- Select a category that matches the item for sale.
- Provide a clear, honest, and accurate description about the item.
- Avoid tactics like keyword spamming because they make it hard for people to find what they're looking for.

Note: Your item description and terms of sale can't be included in an image. They must be in the listing hosted on eBay.

It's against eBay policies to do anything that manipulates the search or browse experience on eBay. This applies to all parts of a listing, including the title, subtitle, product details, description, pictures, links, and meta tags. If you use tactics that can inappropriately divert bidders and buyers to a listing, they can take action.

Before listing items, be sure to read eBay's search and browse manipulation policy to learn more about their guidelines on:

- Brand names
- Categories
- Item details
- Keyword spamming
- Pictures
- Text and other information
- Titles

Other rules include not using profanity in a listing or other community pages on eBay, HTML and JavaScript functions, or links outside of eBay. It's also important to stay in good standing with eBay fee payments. Sometimes sellers try to find ways to get around paying fees or they do so by mistake. Be sure to read their policy about avoiding eBay fees.

You should also read the following policies:

- Profile policy
- No item listings policy
- Tax policy
- Unpaid item abuse policy

Completing the sale

If your item sells, contact your buyer, accept their payment, and post the item.

The above are the basic rules of eBay. It is important that you become acquainted with them. Most are common sense. In the next chapter, we will look at what items to sell on eBay and how best to source those items.

****

Chapter 5

Choosing What Goods to Sell

This book is about buying and selling on eBay. However, although many people will buy an item off eBay and sell it a profit, which is quite common, many more sell items that are sourced elsewhere. We will concentrate on selling goods sourced independent of the site.

Given that eBay sellers sell just about every item under the sun, for a variety of different prices, coming to a decision about what exactly you are going to sell, at a profit, can be difficult. There re a few key decisions that you have to make, quite often the same decisions that any business will have to make, what to sell and where to store it, and at what price to sell?

You should start small by selling things that you own and are surplus to requirements. In the first instance, you are testing your skills as a seller and can hone your approach and perfect techniques such as taking and placing photo's and drawing up effective ads, pricing and postage, going through the whole process from beginning to end.

Small items such as books, DVD's CD's and computer games are ideal. Even small items of unwanted jewellery will sell. These are easy to quantify, to place and it is also easy to see what others arte selling them for. You should concentrate on the UK when starting out, to keep it simple.

Another source of small, inexpensive items that you can buy and easily sell is the car boot sale, or even jumble sales. Like everyone at car boot sales you need to know what will sell, and you will be competing with dealers and traders, doing much the same as you are. Certain rules apply to car boot sales to help you get the right bargains: make sure you get there early, always take plenty of cash, always haggle with the seller so you can ensure profitability when you sell the item on.

Charity shops can reap rewards. It has become obvious over the last few years that charity shops have been transformed (most of them) from flea ridden dumps to attractive retail environments. Oxfam started this trend. In line with this transformation prices have risen. However, it is still very possible to bag a bargain, although haggling is usually out. The location of the shop is important. Shops in posher areas usually have the best cast off's.

Finally, you can go scavenging for stock. Look in skips. It is amazing what people throw away. Look at classified ads sometimes people give things away free to collectors.

However, there will come a time when you will want to move up a league and sell regular stock.

Finding a supplier

You might have followed the above advice and decided to start small, having a few dry runs to see what you can sell and how to perfect your advertising skills. More about this later. However, there will come a time when you want to start making serious money as a seller, which is what this book is all about.

There are ways and means of sourcing stock, and also deciding exactly what it is you want to sell. One of the main ways of deciding what it is you want to sell and also where to get it from is by visiting a Trade Fair. One of the main Trade Fairs is the Spring Fair which is usually held at the beginning of February at the National Exhibition Centre (NEC) near Birmingham. This is massive and has just about everything under the sun, such as jewellery, home wares, sporting equipment, toys and so on. All manufacturers are there and this will give you a lot of inspiration and you can talk to individual suppliers whilst browsing the goods. There is more information about the fair at www.springfair.com

There are other fairs but the NEC fair is by far the most comprehensive. A visit will prove a sound starting block for you and will get you thinking about where you can source goods.

Many people who sell goods will also go to wholesalers and importers of goods. Wholesalers don't usually sell to the public and they sell in volume. It helps if you are a business rather than an individual. There are a number of websites that are very useful when tracking down wholesalers, such as www.wholesaleforum.com/discuss. As the site name suggests this is a forum of wholesalers who can connect you with wholesalers around the world. Another useful site is the Wholesaler at www.thewholesaler.co.uk. There are a number of sites, such as Boffer.co.uk which are wholesalers. At the end of the day it is up to you to research deals which you think might go on to sell for a profit.

Straight to the horses mouth

it is undoubtedly profitable if you can source goods directly from a manufacturer. However, it does tend to be a bit of a closed shop. Manufacturers though, in addition to doing deals with retailers will also do deals with sellers on eBay. Locating manufacturers, particularly overseas can take time. One good site, alibaba.com is useful and deals with goods in Asia, particularly China.

A word of warning about buying goods from overseas: you need to know what you are doing, and about the rules of importing goods, shipping and payments etc. If you have experience here it can certainly provide a profitable source of goods for you.

There are a number of other areas to consider, such as liquidations, auctions and also selling your own wares. Whatever you do, the aim is to ensure that you have sourced the right goods, items that will turn over relatively quickly and are priced correctly.

Selling goods for other people

In addition to sourcing your own stock of goods you could also consider selling other peoples goods, acting as a kind of middleman. What you are essentially doing is taking the hard work out of selling online and taking a commission. If you want to do a bit of background research about this type of service you should visit sites such as stuff u sell at www.stuffusell.co.uk or sell for u at www.sellforyou.co.uk. You can get an idea of charges and how they go about it. Of course, if you are planning a selling career on eBay then you would offer the above type of service as an addition to selling your own goods.

There are many aspects to consider when deciding to sell goods on eBay, not least the management of your capital and storage costs and space generally. Regardless of whether you are selling online or offline, the same business principles will apply. Later on in the book we will be discussing opening your own online store. But before we do that, we will discuss the benefits of opening an eBay shop.

****

Chapter 6

Setting up a Shop on eBay

Why open a store on eBay?

Although you may do well as an individual selling on eBay, by creating an eBay store you can provide a more individual identity, personalise your presence on the site and achieve more sales. Having a shop will also send signals to buyers that you are a serious and organised seller. The following are the key points in favour of opening a shop: more than 17 million unique visitors come to eBay each month to buy a vast range of goods; a Store on eBay can be set-up in a matter of hours; your start-up costs will be low and eBay won't charge you until your first month of trading is complete; payments are received quickly and securely via PayPal so there's no need to apply to Visa etc to take credit cards. As we have seen, although you can take a variety of different payment types, PayPal is the norm; the sales and performance of your store can be easily tracked, using tools available on eBay; any promotions that you decide to run can be set up and used easily from your eBay account

Setting up

To open a new store on eBay you must have a minimum feedback score of 10 on your personal eBay account to open a *basic* store and also be PayPal verified. You must be registered as a business seller to open a *Featured Store* and also have a Detailed Seller Rating of at least 4.4 or above in each of the four areas. If you want to open an *Anchor Shop* your Detailed Seller Rating score must be 4.6 or better.

You also have to consider the costs associated with the type of store you want to open.

Currently costs are:

Basic Shop - £19.99 each month

Featured Shop - £59.99 each month

Anchored Shop - £349.99 each month

These prices are correct as at June 2014. They may vary according to product.

In the following examples we're basing the figures on eBay sellers in general categories. For media and technology sellers, the fees are generally lower.

Basic eBay Shop - £19.99 a Month
Basic shop

If you list a Buy It Now item with no shop it will cost you 40p. With a Basic Shop, the listing fee for business sellers drops to 10p. So if you're listing less than 50 items a month then the listing fees without a shop would be cheaper. If you're listing over 50 items a month then you will pay less in listing fees if you open a Basic Shop.

Featured eBay Shop - £59.99 a Month

The next upgrade level is a Featured Shop. Should you upgrade to a Featured Shop? Buy It Now listings drop to 5p each, making the break-even point 700 for the number of listings. If you regularly list more than 700 items a month, you'd pay less in listing fees by having a Featured Shop. It's also worth noting that the subscription fee for Selling Manager Pro is included with a Featured Shop, making an extra saving of £4.99. If this is something you're already paying for with your Basic Shop, then the break-even point drops to 600 listings.

Anchor eBay Shop - £349.99 a Month

Upgrading to an Anchor Shop gives you Buy It Now listings with no insertion fee, but you need a serious amount of listings to make it worthwhile - 6000 fixed price listings. So if you're listing between 701 and 6000 fixed price listings a month, stick to the Featured Shop. If you have more than 6000 listings, then you'd save money on listing fees by upgrading to an Anchor Shop.

If you're not sure what type of store would suit your business best, eBay has a handy feature comparison chart you can use to help you decide. Also, new businesses that set up on eBay may have listing and selling allowances applied to their store. Ensure you fully understand the possible implication these could have on your new store before you move forward and create your shop.

You also need to carefully consider the on-going running costs in addition to the basic shop cost that are associated with your new store. You have to pay your monthly subscription, but you also need to take into account:

-the listing fees you will pay on each item

-the final value fee that will be applied when a customer buys an item from your store

-the fees that PayPal will charge to process your customer's transaction

What to charge?

For new business on eBay deciding on a pricing strategy can be highly complex. However, the price you charge should take into consideration all the usual fixed and variable costs you would associate with any store.

What you do need to think about is how the price you set impacts on the fees you pay. Don't forget, listing items on your store with a fixed price will attract a fixed listing fee, but also a final value fee that is a percentage of the price you charged with the percentage depending on the category your store's goods are in.

For instance, if you have a Basic Store, your listing fee is £0.10. The final value fee for goods such as computers and video games is 3 per cent. Media such as books and DVDs is 9 per cent, with clothing and accessories costing 12 per cent. These costs should be carefully considered when you are setting the prices for your new eBay store to ensure you get the return you need to ensure a good level of profit.

Design and layout

The first tip here is to take a look on eBay and see what other sellers are offering in terms of design and layout. Also see how they are using their shops. Like many areas of life it may not be necessary to reinvent the wheel.

There are five main areas to consider when building a shop. You need to choose a shop name, choose a design, describe your shop and what you are selling and, very importantly, choose your categories. You will also have to choose key words for search engine optimisation.

It is possible to make your eBay store as simple or complex as you want. Basic templates are available that allow you to choose a design that can then be customised. You can change the colour of your store and add logos and other design elements.

One of the most important aspects of any eBay store is the quality of the images. People who buy on eBay want to see what they are purchasing. The better your images the more sales you will make – it's as simple as that.

Try and make your images as appealing and attractive as possible, and don't forget to optimise them for the web to ensure they download quickly. Customers want pages that load fast, and won't wait for large images to appear. You can even buy third party store templates to use for your new eBay business. Leading services include: Auctiva and Vendio.

As stated above, before you decide how your store will look it's a good idea to take some time and research how other business on eBay that are selling similar items have organised and designed their stores. You need to think about how your store can be designed to standout from the crowd. There are many third-party additions you can make to your store, such as image and photo viewers, that give you more creativity over how your store behaves. By using the right tools you can build a highly attractive eBay store that visitors' will return to again and again.

Ads and promotions

Once your store is live on eBay you can start to promote it. You can use a couple of tools that eBay offers to help you shout about your new business. The first is called the Markdown Manager that allows you to set a discount of between five and 75 per cent that will automatically appear on all items you attach the discount to.

The second service that eBay offers is their email newsletter. Your store can have an option to 'sign up for store newsletter'. The tool allows you to create newsletters that can be used to promote your store to everyone that has expressed an interest in hearing more about your store and business.

Outside of the tools that eBay offers, you can use a wide range of promotional activity to drive customers to your eBay store. If you already have a website, linking to your eBay store for exclusive discounts can be highly effective.

You could also use ad services such as Google's Adwords, and you should also make your eBay store search engine friendly. This simply means making sure your store loads quickly into your visitor's browser and that you have used the appropriate keywords in the text your pages contain so that anyone using Google or any other search engine will see your store.

Your checklist

Follow this checklist to ensure you set up your eBay store properly and give it the best chance of success:

-Do your research to see how other businesses in your sector are using eBay. Ask yourself what you can do better?

-Ensure the design of your store is engaging and professional. Make sure your text is search engine friendly and that each image is attractive and optimised for the web

-Look closely at all the costs associated with your business before deciding on the prices you will charge

-A good reputation is vital on eBay – some people won't buy from stores with a low positive comments percentage. Deal with problems quickly and efficiently to protect your business' reputation

-Track every aspect of your store to see what is working and what needs to be changed. Stores that are updated regularly make more sales

-Use the social media networks including Facebook and Twitter to make personal connections with your existing and potential customers

* * * * * * * * * * * * * * *

Chapter 7

The Legal Rights of the Buyer of Goods on eBay

As we have seen, eBay provides a marketplace for thousands of online buyers and sellers. The way a person buys affects their legal rights and whether they are covered by the Distance Selling Regulations 2000. These vary depending on whether they are buying from an individual or a business, and whether they win an auction or have bought at an agreed price from a seller. PayPal also has it own dispute resolution process. The principles in law apply whether you are buying from eBay or Amazon or any other site. The only difference is that each site will have their own buyer protection policies.

eBay - Consumer rights buying from a business-eBay auctions

If a person buys something in an auction from a business on eBay, then it's unlikely they will be able to complain about the item they receive unless the goods are not as described by the seller. A person should make enquiries about the condition of the goods and make sure they are fit for their particular purpose before bidding on them.

The Distance Selling Regulations 2000 (DSRs) don't apply to goods bought at an auction so a buyer has no automatic right to return an item if they are the highest bidder and they change their mind. Buyers should check the seller's terms of sale to see if they have voluntarily agreed to accept returns and what that returns policy is.

The seller can set a reserve price which they are not obliged to disclose – if the reserve is not met the buyer can't force the seller to sell the item to them.

Buy it Now

Many sellers will set a 'Buy it Now' price which a buyer may think is worth paying if there's an item they really want and don't want to run the risk of losing out on in an auction. In practice the seller is offering two different ways of buying the same item.

While the item bought through the auction wouldn't be covered by the Distance Selling Regulations, it could be covered if they bought it from a business using the 'Buy it Now' option. The item would only be excluded from cover if it was an item the Distance Selling Regulations don't apply to, such as something that was personalised for them, or items such as CDs or DVDs which have been opened.

But because the buyer is purchasing from a business they would have the protection of the Sale of Goods Act 1987 if the goods weren't of satisfactory quality, fit for purpose or as described.

Make me an offer

Some sellers offer a third option which enables the buyer to put forward a price that they would be happy to pay. If the seller accepts this offer then a contract is created and, as with 'Buy it Now' purchases, the contract would be covered by the Sale of Goods Act and the Distance Selling Regulations - unless the item is one that the Distance Selling Regulations don't apply to, or that the buyer doesn't have the right to cancel.

eBay - Rights buying from an individual

Many individuals will sell unwanted gifts or items that they no longer need. Here the buyer is purchasing from a private seller in the same way as if they were buying from a classified advert in a local paper, and the principle of 'buyer beware' applies. When a buyer purchases from an individual, the Sale of Goods Act says that the goods they get must be as they were described to them. For example, something second-hand should not be described as new - if it is, the seller will be in breach of contract. If a seller takes the buyer's money, but then sends nothing they would again be in breach of contract.

Some people who sell through eBay may be doing so much business that they are considered traders rather than individuals. In this situation the buyer would have the same rights as if they bought from a business, but they would have to find evidence that the seller is indeed a business if they wanted to make a claim against them as a business seller.

eBay Buyer Protection

eBay offers it's own dispute resolution process. But there are some conditions that need to be met which include:

- the claim must be submitted within 45 days of payment for the goods
- the buyer must have paid through PayPal and into the seller's PayPal account. If they haven't they can still submit a claim and eBay will try to resolve the issue with the seller
- they must have made only one payment and sent that payment using the 'Pay Now' button
- the item mustn't be on the list of excluded purchases. These include items purchased from classified ads and vehicles including cars and motorbikes.

The buyer can use eBay Buyer Protection if the item was significantly different from its description or it was broken or didn't work in the way that had been described.

In both cases the buyer must have raised the issue with the seller and given them three days to respond. They can also use the process if they didn't receive the goods within three days of the estimated delivery date, or if a delivery date isn't given within seven days of making payment. The seller can either dispute the claim, offer a refund or a replacement, or send the original if it was never delivered. If the seller doesn't respond or doesn't accept the claim they can ask eBay for a resolution. If the seller said they would provide a refund or a replacement, and more than five days have passed since the seller has received the item you sent back, they can also ask eBay for a resolution.

If eBay upholds the claim, it can process a refund which will be made as a PayPal credit. eBay Buyer Protection also applies to counterfeit goods. If the goods are found to be fake, eBay can require the buyer to destroy them.

PayPal Buyer Protection

PayPal also has its own dispute resolution process called PayPal Buyer Protection which the buyer can choose to use instead of eBay Buyer Protection. This can also be used if they make a Paypal purchase from a trader that wasn't operating through eBay. It's very similar to eBay Buyer Protection in that a claim can be made in the same circumstances and payment must have been made in specified ways.

As with eBay Buyer Protection, a dispute must be opened within 45 days of payment but certain items aren't covered, such as motorbikes and cars. If the buyer and the seller can't resolve the dispute, the dispute must be escalated to a claim within 20 days of lodging the dispute. If PayPal finds in the buyer's favour, it can order the seller to refund the original cost of the item and the postage paid. But the buyer would be responsible for the cost of returning it to the seller.

****

Chapter 8

International Sales

Selling on eBay is fun and can be tremendously profitable in your own country, but one of the most unique aspects of the eBay marketplace is its truly international nature. Through eBay, buyers and sellers can complete transactions from different countries and areas of the world, buying and selling in different currencies—in the same transaction.

Although around 17 million people in the United Kingdom visit eBay each month, the sites global reach exceeds 300 million. Therefore, it goes without saying that not selling internationally can severely restrict your potential.

It is also true that as the main markets, including the UK, are slowing down there are important emerging markets, such as Brazil, Russia, India and China (BRICS) that are rapidly expanding. Therefore, when setting up your business, keep your eye in this direction.

Posting an International Listing

Posting an international listing on eBay is easy and can be done from the standard selling form. In the "Give buyers shipping details" area of the form (located on the same page on which you describe your item), perform the following steps to set up international shipping:

o Click on the box initially marked "No international shipping" to open a drop-down list giving you international options.

o Select either "Flat: same cost to all buyers" if you want to charge a single shipping rate to all of the locations you're willing to shop to, or select "Calculated: cost varies by buyer location" to enter shipping costs for each different location to which you're willing to ship.

o Use the rest of that part of the form, including the "Ship to" and "Services" drop-down lists, to add shipping destinations and costs one by one, or select "Worldwide" if you're willing to ship worldwide.

By selecting international shipping locations and costs, you've told eBay that you're willing to sell to people in those areas, and eBay will show your auction listing to international buyers accordingly.

Before you start selling to international buyers, accepting payments from them, and shipping goods to them, there are a number of things you should be aware of as a seller. By keeping these issues in mind, you can reduce considerably any hassles that might otherwise arise during the exchange.

You're not actually listing on international eBay sites. There's a difference between selling to international buyers that are shopping on your home country's eBay site and actually posting a listing on an eBay site in another country. If you live in the United States but your intent is to reach the widest possible swath of buyers in Hong Kong, for example, you might want to actually list your item on eBay's Hong Kong website, rather than merely opening bidding to Hong Kong-based shoppers on the United States eBay site. Be prepared, however, to list in another language if you're this serious about international selling.

Select areas carefully. When you say you'll ship "worldwide" (as opposed to only selecting certain areas of the globe), you're agreeing to do business with literally anyone on the planet, including areas that can present a higher-than-average amount of trouble to sellers (some parts of eastern Europe, for example, as the result of alarmingly high levels of credit card fraud). If you're new to international trade, start slowly; if you're an American seller, for example, begin with the United Kingdom, Canada, and Australia you're more familiar with the process and more able to spot and manage problem buyers and items.

PayPal is easier by far. Accepting international payments can be a hassle. In worst case scenarios, it can actually lose you money or get you involved with unsavory characters. Apart from currency conversions there are problems with credit card fraud, bank fees, delays in sending and receiving checks by mail, and so on. PayPal remains by far the easiest way to send and receive international payments, since it is fast and converts currency at reasonable exchange rates for you and your buyer automatically.

Be an informed shipper. International shipping can be a nightmare, especially if you're unfamiliar with the process or with the services offered by the shipper you select. Select a shipper that will have some measure of control over the process (or at least minimal trackability) all the way to a package's destination in the country at issue. Make clear to buyers that you won't lie on customs forms about shipment content or value, since this may lead to seizure or additional taxes and tariffs at customs checkpoints. If you are a seller that habitually uses "flat rate" or "free" shipping, keep in mind, too, that international shipping can cost anywhere from 2-5 times more than domestic shipping, depending on destination and package size.

Communicate clearly. Because differences in native languages can increase the potential for misunderstanding, it is extremely important that you communicate clearly when selling internationally. Use simple, strong language in your listing and email communication and include as many high-quality photos in your listing as possible. If there is any doubt in your mind that your trading partner understands an important aspect of the transaction, follow up with them and ask them to confirm that they understand you.

Beware of customs costs. Both you and your buyer need to be aware of any extra costs that may be incurred as the item in question goes through customs in the destination country so that you can make arrangements with one another about who will pay such fees and how they are to be paid.

Be mindful of the laws in the destination country. Some types of goods are prohibited in some countries and/or prevented from crossing its borders. Before you make a sale and ship an item, be sure that both you and your trading partner know the item's legal status in its destination country.

By keeping these points in mind you can increase the likelihood of a happy, successful, and trouble-free transaction for both you and your international trading partner(s). More information about international eBay trading, including about local rules and laws for each eBay site, can be found on eBay's international trading help page.

****

Chapter 9

Reasons for Failure as an eBay seller

A summary of the The Main reasons eBay businesses fail

Building an eBay business is similar to building any business. You need business acumen in order to be successful. You need effective Marketing, Sales, Quality, Pricing, and Customer Service. However, there are obviously some differences between conventional businesses and eBay models.

On eBay, a seller's customer service reputation (Feedback Rating) is out in the open for everyone to see. This is not the case with conventional business. Negative feedback is the number one reason eBay sellers fail. A negative feedback rating, however, usually has its roots in other problems inherent in the business and below we will examine each problem in turn.

Poor Feedback Rating

New eBay sellers typically under-rate the importance of quickly building a great feedback rating. Experienced eBay bidders are understandably cautious of sellers, whether with a store or individual seller, with a feedback rating under 25 - 50. Obtaining your first twenty-five feedback comments as a seller can be a long process. As we have seen earlier in the book, before you rush into selling on eBay, you need to get some experience buying. There is nothing better than putting yourself in your customers' shoes.

When starting your eBay business, you should try very hard indeed to provide exceptional service. When you have a positive feedback rating over 100, bidders will look at your rating number and then make their decision on whether or not they like your product. If your feedback rating is less than a 100, people tend to actually look back through your comments and read them.

Poor communications between buyer and seller is the leading cause of negative feedback. Make sure your first email to the successful bidder is clear, and complete. You should not only be polite, but be effusive in your congratulations. Remember, some people shop on eBay for bargains, but most people shop on eBay for fun. Make the transaction a fun experience. Be personal. Make the buyer feel good and complete the sale by complimenting them on the great deal they made.

Make sure your payment instructions are crystal clear and your shipping methods and charges are clearly spelled out. If a buyer wants to pay by credit card, suggest PayPal, or explain how to access your secure credit card server. If they want to use a check, explain how they can speed up the payment and delivery by using PayPal's electronic check service.

Anything you can do to speed up payment, shortens the time it takes a customer to receive their purchase. Nothing will improve your feedback faster than getting purchases to your customers quickly.

Weak Headlines and Poor Auction Descriptions Lose Bids

The above two elements are very important in the process of promoting your wares on eBay. This is, essentially, all to do with the design and layout of your shop or, if you dont have a shop, of your individual adverts.

There are millions of items listed on eBay every day. Your headline must stand out above the competition to attract bidders. A strong headline should contain two key elements: **Key words** that are searchable, and **emotional** words designed to attract attention.

A high percentage of bidders find the item they are looking for by using the Search feature. Unless you use the key words bidders are looking for, you will miss many bids.

Your headline should also include emotional words designed to attract a bidder's attention. These words should include 'new, rare, unique, sexy, unbelievable, great-value, etc. However, you should not call something --rare-- if it is not. But, there are other adjectives that work well in headlines. Besides the emotional words you can use words such as exquisite, charming, wonderful, mint, perfect, clean, superb, etc. Just make sure you are accurate.

Once you catch the bidder's attention with a great headline, you need to sell them with your item description. Too many bidders simply describe the item they are selling. You must sell the benefits of buying your item.

Before writing the auction description, ask yourself: --Why would someone want to own the item you are selling.-- If you are selling something you use, say so. Tell the potential bidder why you owned the item, how you used it, what benefits it brought you. Sell not just the features, but the benefits and the romance.

Your auction descriptions must also be complete. A clear photo is critical to the success of the auction, but remember, photos don't always show all the details a bidder needs. If you are selling an antique, collectible or any used item, be sure to describe any and all flaws. The fastest way to build negative feedback is to over-describe the item, or over-promise performance.

Poor Images

A poor image will obviously turn away buyers. Not having a photo of your item will greatly reduce your bids, and lead to unprofitable or unsuccessful auctions. Not only must you have a photograph of what you are selling, the photo must be accurate and revealing.

It is not necessary to be a professional photographer. eBay bidders understand that most sellers are taking snapshots of the products they sell. But, your photo should be clear, and show the product as completely as possible.

Not understanding your costs

This is a certain prescription for disaster. It is so easy for a new seller to get caught up in the process of selling and not pay attention to the actual costs involved in selling. Before deciding whether to sell an item on eBay, and what to sell it for, you will need to make 100 percent certain that you understand all the costs involved.

First of all there is the listing fee. There is also a selling fee that will be set by what price the item actually sells for. There may be a fee to process a Bill-Point, PayPal or credit card sale. If you use an auction management service then you have their fees. Very Importantly, don't forget postage, and the cost of the materials involved in postage.

If you are selling items you purchased wholesale, were there postage charges to get it to you? Did you pay VAT on the item?

Many businesses fail because they are either under financed, or because they do not understand their costs. An appropriate software programme would be a good investment which will allow you to track all costs involved.

You can get an idea of what software is available by visiting eBay, who have a number of suggestions. You can also access different software online.

Vist the eBay university

Reading a book such as this one, or any other publication, should help to get you started on the path to successful online trading. However, If you are still uncertain about any aspect of eBay and this is leading to problems that are affecting your business, then if you are serious about building an eBay business, it's absolutely key that you learn not only to use the site properly, but also how to use it most effectively. One way of doing that learning is through eBay University, which is a learning program that eBay established to help people become successful eBay merchants.

There are two courses that you should be considering:

1. The "Selling Basics" course, which will teach you how to open a seller's account, how to conduct research and create listings, how to

improve listings for greater success, how to integrate PayPal with eBay, how to monitor your auctions, and how to complete transactions.

2. The "Beyond the Basics" course: You will need to complete "Selling Basics", before you are ready for this more advanced course. In "Beyond the Basics", you will discover how to start and grow an eBay business, how to choose and create listing formats that sell, how to use all of the eBay resources, how to market your business, how to pack and ship your items, and much more.

Both courses are reasonably priced, and well worth the short amount of time that it takes to complete each course. As well benefiting from the actual information imparted, they will also help boost your confidence, allowing you to become not only more successful, but a more assured eBay seller too.

eBay university can be accessed through the eBay site.

****

Chapter 10

Selling Goods on Amazon

---

amazon.com

There is one main difference between eBay and Amazon and that is that the Amazon marketplace, which is huge, sells mainly, (but not exclusively), new goods. Although there are a few second hand goods, you would definitely struggle to make a living from selling them.

Although Amazon is best known for books and music, and other media, if you look at the Amazon site you will see that they sell a wide range of articles and Amazon is developing its categories all the time.

The other major difference is that Amazon is itself a retailer, runs warehouses, and sends out goods. It has a number of massive warehouses dotted around, notably in Milton Keynes. eBay is not a retailer, eBay brings people together to create the market place whereas Amazon will operate in competition with you. So saying that, almost 40% and rising of sales on Amazon are by third party sellers.

When you use Amazon as a base to sell your goods, there is a lot less opportunity to personalise your wares as you will incorporate pre-prepared descriptions into your listings. For example, when you sell something, you simply put in the EAN (barcode) number (more later) into the site and Amazon will fill in the details. Although this makes Amazon easy to use it reduces the opportunity for you to stand out from other sellers.

One of the best ways to stand out on Amazon is to ensure that you are cheaper than the rest. Amazon will display products in a way that favour cheaper items. When it comes to postage however, for a number of products, such as music and books, postage costs are determined by Amazon so you can't use postage as a competitive edge. See more about Amazon fulfilment at the end of the chapter.

Registering on Amazon

When you sell on Amazon UK, you will only be able to sell goods on the UK site. You will need to choose which package suits you best. there are two packages, Basic and Pro. If you are selling few items on the site you will probably go for the basic which costs 75p per listing. You will also pay item selling fees.

If you anticipate selling many items you will go for the Pro which attracts a subscription of £25 per month but has no listing fees, although you will pay commission on sales. There are a few more perks to the Pro package. More selling categories are available, you can access the bulk listing and tracking tools that Amazon offers and you have the chance to be a featured seller. Basically, as with everything, the more you pay the more you get.

As a Pro customer, you can take advantage of the Amazon 'Jump Start' programme. This means that Amazon staff will prepare your Amazon listings following Amazon's best practice guidelines. A minimum of 100 listings is needed to benefit from the service. This kind of service will make the subscription very worthwhile as it will save you an awful lot of time and get you up and running very quickly. You will see the following message displayed.

Sell on Amazon with Jumpstart

Sign up as a Pro seller
Register your Marketplace seller account to get started

Email us details of your catalogue
We will assess your listing needs and contact you for more detailed product information

Review your Amazon listings
Review your catalogue to ensure your offers are correct before they go live

Start selling
Start selling on your chosen platforms: Amazon.co.uk, Amazon.de, Amazon.fr, Amazon.it or Amazon.es

---

What you need to get started

As with eBay, there are certain requirements to get started on Amazon.

Set up your Seller Central account

Create your account

Seller Central is the name of the application for Sellers on Amazon. You can access your account at https://sellercentral-europe.amazon.com. If you do not have an account yet, you can register at http://www.amazon.co.uk/promerchant.

Enter name and address

During the registration process you are asked to provide both your business name, which will be shown on the Amazon site, and your legal name and address, which is stored in your account for Amazon's reference. If you are a registered company, it is important to use the exact name and address under which you are registered. You can change this information on the "Account Info" page under the "Settings" tab in Seller Central.

Enter VAT number

If you are a VAT registered business, input your VAT number when you create your Seller Central account. After registration, you can enter it on the "Account Info" page under the "Settings" tab. If you are not VAT registered or do not input your VAT number, you will be charged VAT on your Amazon seller fees.

Enter bank account information

Your Amazon sales funds will be disbursed to your bank account once every 14 days from the day you set up your payments account. To set up your payments account, you need a bank account based in one of the supported countries (see list of supported countries on the site). If you use a bank account in Euros to sell on Amazon.co.uk or a bank account in British Pounds to sell on Amazon.de or Amazon.fr you have to agree to the Terms and Conditions of the Amazon Currency Converter TM for Sellers service. You can edit your bank account information on the "Account Info" page.

Enter credit card information

When you create your Amazon account, you will need to provide valid credit card information. Your monthly subscription fee will be charged to this credit card when you create your account. This card will also be charged if in future months your sales revenue is less than the monthly subscription fee. You can edit your credit card details on the "Account Info" page.

Set your shipping rates

Accurate shipping information is critical for a good customer experience. You should define the location from which you ship, the countries you ship to, and your shipping rates. Amazon sets the shipping rates for Books, Music, Video, and DVD (BMVD) to provide a consistent buying experience from all sellers in these categories. For all other items you have the choice of three pricing structures: weight-based shipping, item-based shipping, and price-banded shipping. You can set your shipping prices on the "Shipping Settings" page under the "Settings" tab. You should refer to Seller Central help for details on the different shipping pricing structures. (see Amazon fulfilment below).

Set up your information and policies

To provide customers with information about your returns process, shipping service, and customer service, you have to fill in the "Your Info & Policies" page under the "Settings" tab. Please note that you cannot include a URL or link to your web store in your information. This would be a breach of your Selling on Amazon Agreement.

Amazon recommends that you fill in the "About Seller" and "Returns & Refunds" sections. Please bear in mind that you are responsible for complying with all applicable laws with respect to both your listings as well as the information displayed in your Seller Profile. they also recommend that you upload your seller logo. This makes it easier to identify you as a merchant to customers when they have the choice between several offers. Your logo must be 120x30 pixels in size and may not contain a reference to your own web store. Finally, you may want to use the "Custom Help Pages" section to provide general information related to your offers, such as shoe sizing charts.

Choose the best listing method for you

Amazon.co.uk offers you different methods for listing your products and for managing your inventory. You need to decide which listing method works best for you.

If you want to sell only few products (up to 50), you can add them using the Seller Central "**Add a Product**" page.

If you sell many Books, Media, Video, or DVD products which are already in the Amazon catalogue, you should use the **Inventory Loader** file template. It uses ISBN or bar codes to create your listings and can be downloaded from Seller Central.

If you sell many other products which are already in the Amazon catalogue, you can use the **Listings Loader**, which is a simple template that uses bar codes or ASINs to create your listings. This template is in Excel format and can be downloaded from Seller Central.

If you sell multiple products (more than 50) which are not yet in the Amazon catalogue, they recommend you use the **Inventory File** which corresponds to your main product category. You can download these templates from Seller Central. If you create new product pages, you will have to follow the instructions below on how to prepare your product information for best results.

If you choose to upload your listings through one of the Excel templates, once you have created your inventory file, save it as a tab delimited text file. You can find this option when you chose the *Save As* option under the *File* menu and chose *text (tab delimited)*.

It is recommended that you first upload less than twenty products, to get the method right. Once these have uploaded without errors, you can upload your entire inventory. Generally the listing will happen within minutes, You should allow up to 24 hours for your listing to appear on Amazon.

Prepare your product information

On Amazon.co.uk, each product has its own page with detailed information, customer reviews, and more. They call this a Product Detail Page. When you add your own product information on Amazon.co.uk, this information will appear on the Product Detail Page. Your price, quantity, and condition constitute your offer for selling that product.

Product information and offer information are separate, and offers from multiple merchants may be associated to a single product. This is why you must not enter any offer related information to your product descriptions. To make sure you create compelling product pages, please follow the category style guides which contain detailed instructions and examples.

Barcode requirements

You need bar codes to create new products on Amazon. The following bar code standards are supported:

ISBN (International Standard Book Number) – a 10 digit international standard

UPC (Universal Product Code) – a 12 digit US-American standard

EAN (European Article Number) – a 13 digit European standard. EAN-8 with 8 digits is also supported

GTIN (Global Trade Identification Number) – a 14 digit global standard

Barcodes consist of only numbers without any space. If you do not have barcodes for your products, you should ask the manufacturer of your products to provide you with barcodes. If you are the manufacturer, you can buy barcodes at http://gs1uk.org. Finally, if your products are already sold on Amazon, you can use the ASIN (Amazon Standard Identification Number) to create new offers on these products. The ASIN is displayed on each product detail page.

Product title requirements

Your product titles are essential to helping customers discover your products and should describe your products as concisely as possible. Do not include offer-related information in the product title (i.e. pricing, promotion, name of the shop etc.).

Product search terms

Many customers use the Amazon product search to find products. You should add 5 relevant keywords to each of your items to help customers find them. Title, EAN or UPC, manufacturer and seller are automatically added to the search terms. So you don't have to enter them manually. Search terms are not available on the BMVD templates.

Amazon product classification

One key to successful selling on Amazon is properly categorising your products, so that customers find them when browsing. You can do so by assigning browse nodes to your products. These define the places within the Amazon store where your products will be displayed. Think of the browse node as an aisle and shelf in a store. If a product is in the wrong aisle on the wrong shelf, it is unlikely to be found and purchased by the customer.

You can download browse tree guides with lists of valid browse nodes from the "Browse Tree Guides" section in the Seller Central help. Always use the most specific browse node for any given product.

Be very aware of customer experience

It is important that you know how to handle orders efficiently to deliver the best possible customer experience. Poor order handling will result in negative customer feedback and A-Z guarantee claims, which in turn will have a severe impact on your business on Amazon. Amazon expect 99% of orders to meet a customers' expectations both in term of product satisfaction and delivery experience. If your performance is consistently below 99% positive, your account and selling privileges will be at risk.

Check for orders daily

You have several order notification options – email and/or order report. You can enable email order notifications on the "Account Info" page under the "Settings" tab. In addition, an order report can be scheduled and downloaded from Seller Central in the "Orders" tab. Amazon recommend you check your orders at least daily to make sure nothing gets lost.

Confirm when you ship

When you have dispatched an order, you will need to confirm that you have shipped this product in Seller Central. Your confirmation triggers a shipping confirmation email to the customer and charges their credit card. Your account will not be credited until you confirm the shipment.

You can confirm shipments in Seller Central one-by-one under the "Orders" tab or in bulk by using a flat file. The shipping confirmation flat file can be downloaded and uploaded on the "Upload Order Related Files" page under the "Orders" tab.

Control your Order Defect Rate to avoid suspension

The Seller Performance Scorecard, located under the "Reports" tab, is intended to give you a summary of how you are doing with respect to customer satisfaction. It indicates whether or not you're meeting Amazon's performance expectations with regard to order defect, cancellation and late ship rates. Your performance in each of those areas is summarised as good, fair, or poor. Order Defect Rate is the key measure of a seller's ability to provide customer satisfaction. If you're not meeting Amazon's target for order defect rate and do not improve, your account may be suspended and their Seller Performance team may ask you to provide a detailed "plan of action" in which you explain the source of the problem and how you have corrected it.

Build a good feedback rating
Customer feedback is taken very seriously by Amazon, as it is with eBay and is fundamental to maintaining a safe and trusted selling

platform. Your customer feedback statistics are available under the "Reports" tab. Amazon recommends that you monitor feedback closely making ongoing adjustments to improve your customer satisfaction. Contact any customer who left negative feedback and try to resolve the cause of their dissatisfaction. When communicating with customers, please remember to always stay courteous regardless of their conduct.

Manage refunds

If required, Seller Central provides you with the option to issue either a full or partial refund. Partial refunds are useful where a customer ordered several products and one product suddenly becomes unavailable. With the customers consent, you can refund the part for the missing product and still ship the remaining products.

Check your inventory regularly

Keep an eye on quantity of inventory you have in stock – especially if you sell through multiple channels. Customers who submit orders for products that turn out to not be in stock are likely to leave negative feedback. If you get into this situation, the best move is to quickly inform the customer and, if appropriate, cancel the order.

Be accessible to customers

Nothing is more frustrating to a customer than not knowing the status of their order. Please respond quickly to customer contacts and notify them when an order is delayed. Make it easy for customers to know how to reach you so that they trust that you will make their sales experience go smoothly.

Know where to look for answers

Take time to examine all the tools on Seller Central as well as your Selling on Amazon Agreement and our other policies. If you have questions, a good place to begin is the Seller Central *Help* link located in the upper right hand corner of the page. You can also contact technical support by following the Contact Seller Support link at the bottom of each seller central page.

A few words about Amazon

The Amazon site is very user friendly. As you are registering and launching your products there are links such as 'Learn More' which offer advice each step of the way.

Amazon fulfilment

For any of you who have ever bought goods from Amazon, you will know that they have a really efficient set up when it comes to fulfilment. Amazon offer these services to merchants at a price through a service called Fulfilment by Amazon. It is quite simple to use: you send your goods to an Amazon warehouse and it stores them for you. When they are sold they will pick and pack for you at the prevailing postage rate.

Its an excellent service and is well worth the fee as this is another aspect of the business that can be expensive and time consuming if you do it yourself.

Amazon claims that FBA customers see a 30-40% uplift in sales because the programme comes with some advantages:

o   Eligibility for free Super Saver Delivery and Amazon Prime for FBA listings on Amazon.co.uk

o   Use of the 'Fulfilled by Amazon' message making your FBA listings more attractive to buyers

o   The ability to sell on the French, German and Italian Amazon marketplaces from a single inventory pool in the UK.

You should consider the costs carefully and see if they are going to be worthwhile. There is a warehousing fee for every month your goods are stored and also an FBA fee on top of this plus the Pro selling fees. In total, fees might add up to 30% of the sales price. There is a download that explains the FBA fees at: amazon.com/images/g/02/images/FBA_UK_RateCard_EN_ratecard:pdf.

For more about FBA generally, go to:
www.amazon.co.uk/gp/help/customer/display.

****

Chapter 11

Selling Goods on Other Sites

There are a number of other auction and sales sites which have developed in the wake of the major two, eBay and Amazon. Although you will no doubt start your selling career on one or both of the major two, it is well worth taking a look at the other sites that are out there.

The first, obvious alternative to the two giants is another giant, facebook. There is ample opportunity to create a selling platform and the procedure for selling on facebook is laid out very clearly on facebook itself and also on sites such as www.wikihow.com.

There are a number of other smaller sites and the ones listed below are a selection of the popular alternative sites. It is entirely up to you whether you decide to use one or more of them, but they can provide food for thought.

PlayTrade

PlayTrade is an alternative way to make money selling your DVDs, CDs, Books, Games and more to the millions of customers who shop at Play.com. As a PlayTrade seller, your products will appear for sale on the Play.com web site, giving you the benefits that only the UK's largest entertainment online retailer can offer. They do all the advertising and merchandising, credit card processing and first-line customer care. All you need to do is decide on your price and send the products to the customers promptly. PlayTrade also offer ProTrader accounts where sellers can list gadgets, electronics and PC items on top of the usual media products, giving you access to the API plus a number of other benefits all for a monthly fee.

Address: http://www.play.com

CQout.com

CQout is an International online market place and auction community. It was launched in Dec 1999 and has since gained the reputation of the "Most Trusted Online Auction Site". CQout also claims to be the "2nd biggest auction site" based on the number of active listings, and reaching into 80 countries around the globe. A membership fee is required for all buyers and sellers, but standard listings are free and final value fees are competitive. As all members are individually verified, CQout is one of the most trustworthy online selling sites to use and incorporates its own secure payment handling system with 100% buyer and seller protection. CQout also offer a one to one customer service helpline.

Address: http://www.cqout.com

eBid.net

International auction site eBid donï charge listing fees and you're only charged a small final value fee when your item sells. 5 Free photos are included in every eBid listing, and for a flat fee sellers can enjoy unlimited listings and no final value fees for the life of their account! Up to 5 stores can be opened and operated for sellers and a bulk upload facility is offered to enable fast import of inventory. With over 3 million listings on eBid, there is plenty of choice for buyers, and nearly 10,000 categories gives sellers plenty of choice. Secure payments are made and received through either Paypal, PPPay or Google Checkout.

Address: http://www.ebid.net

Gumtree.com
Gumtree is the #1 website in the UK for free classified advertising. Standard adverts are free to place and there are no fees to pay upon the completion of the sale. This is essentially the same as advertising in your local newspaper, all transactions are completed between the buyer and seller, with no intervention from Gumtree. Sellers can advertise on their local city network, and with 50 major UK cities and counties listed, Gumtree has full UK coverage. And it is not just for selling your unwanted goods or browsing for bargains; Gumtree also lists homes for sale, job opportunities, local businesses and even lonely hearts!

Address: http://www.gumtree.com

Webidz.com
Webidz was introduced in 2005, and despite a slow start, it now has a large amount of regular sellers and buyers along with thousands of active auctions and listings. They offer zero fees on all auctions with a choice of featured upgrades from just a few dollars. A registration fee is required for all new sellers, which could be seen as a downfall,

however, this keeps scammers and fakes away from the website as the fee is used to verify seller accounts. Address: http://www.webidz.com

eCRATER.com

eCRATER is both a free web store builder and a free online marketplace. If you are a seller you can create your own free online store in minutes. If you are a buyer you can browse and search among millions of products. All products are submitted to the Google Product Search and if you adding eCRATER as a secondary site to eBay then you can easily import your eBay products as well. They are definitely one of the places buyers and sellers turn to when they eventually determine they have had enough with eBay and their constant rising fees.

Address: http://www.ecrater.com

Vivastreet.co.uk

Vivastreet is the 2nd largest classified advertising website in the UK and is 100% free. They cover more than 70 selling categories, from Cars and bikes, to jobs, property and household goods for sale, as well as local services and educational classes. Buyers and sellers can deal direct with each other via email, chat or Vivastreet secure messaging. Sellers can post one advert every 2 minutes, and the same ad in the same category every 48 hours.

Address: http://www.vivastreet.co.uk

Preloved.co.uk

Preloved is an online classified advertising website, covering the whole of the UK & Ireland. It was founded in 1998 and has many thousands of second hand items for sale in over 500 categories. What makes Preloved unique is the opportunity it provides for enthusiasts and collectors to gather together as a community.

Address: http://www.preloved.co.uk

Specialistauctions.com

Established in late 2005, specialistauctions.com is a trading division of Vujoo Ltd.

The whole concept of Vujoo and therefore SpecialistAuctions, is based around communities. Communities whether they are established sporting clubs, collecting groups or people with special interests. The concept revolves around leveraging the support within these communities and creating a safe and cost effective environment where communities can interact. In SpecialistAuctions case, enabling buying and selling between each other.

Address. www.specialistauctions.com

Priceminister.co.uk

PriceMinister is one of the main European online marketplaces. PriceMinister targets the UK, French and Spanish markets with more than 170 million products. The site offers the largest selection of DVDs, CDs, books, video games, fashion and high tech products in Europe at the lowest prices. PriceMinister acts as a trusted third party between buyers and sellers, and guarantees that transactions are carried out quickly, securely and trouble-free. There are no postage charges for buyers, and listings are free for sellers, who also receive a post and packing rebate from PriceMinister

Address: http://www.priceminister.co.uk

iBootSale.co.uk

Just like a car boot sale, where you would add your unwanted possessions to your pitch for others to browse, haggle and purchase. At iBootSale the principle is the same, the only two limits are the size and duration of your pitch. One simple charge for pitch hire (currently FREE!), no hidden fees or percentages costs etc. Buyers can join, browse, haggle and purchase completely FREE of charge. Sellers can take advantage of our FREE 90 day pitch at iBootSale. Sell 25 up to items completely free of charges or fees. Larger pitches are periodically offered to users with well stocked pitches.

Address: http://www.iBootSale.co.uk

Sellmyretro.com

SellMyRetro.com is a new trading place to bring enthusiasts and traders of retro computers, gaming machines and other electronics equipment together in one place. Listing and final value fees apply, although you can open a store free of charge which simply directs people back to your own personal website; enabling free advertising. Stores within this site are charged a monthly fee and come with a 50% reduction in fees.

Address:http://www.sellmyretro.com

flogitall.com

This has to be one of the more unique auction sites, here's a qoute from the owner..."This is a not for profit service intended for use by anyone wishing to use it. As the owner of the site I make no charges whatsoever for anyone wishing to use the site" I've used the site myself and it's true, there's nothing whatsoever to pay in fees, from what i can gather the owner has set up the site as a hobby and intends to make no profit whatsoever, thee site is also free from any revenue making adverts! Maybe he has more money than sense or maybe it's the future. Either way you have nothing to lose so give it a try.

Address: http://www.flogitall.com

Totalbids.co.uk

Totalbids is the UK's completely free online auction site where you can sign up, buy, sell and even open your own store free of charge. The site has quite a few regular sellers and a decent amount of traffic, it still has a very long way to go in order to compete with some of the busier sites but the design is unique, clean and manageable, definitely worth a try!
.
Address: http://www.totalbids.co.uk

LGG Auctions

LGGauctions aim to cater for the new breed of Auction user. They function well with speed and security, ensuring your online auction experience is as enjoyable and safe as possible. Registration is free.

Address: http://www.lggauctions.co.uk

87

Kickoff3pm.com

The site has many features that will help both buyers and sellers of football items. The site policy is based around security and durability, and apart from the football auction they also provide a way to list your wanted items. If you prefer not to deal with money we also have an exchange system and for those who just want to express themselves they provide a free football blog server.

Address: http://www.kickoff3pm.com

Bid-ALot.co.uk

BidaLot.co.uk is a Non Profit online auction website. The site has been online since 2004 & was started in order to help the general public have a place to sell their items for - FREE. Not many listings but a good number of members so could be worth keeping an eye on.

Address: http://www.bid-alot.co.uk

****

88

Chapter 12

Using Multi-Channel Software

What does multi-channel mean?

There are a lot of companies out there offering multi-channel software and multi-channel marketing opportunities. What does it all mean though?

As the name suggest, each avenue through which you are trying to sell your goods is called a channel. the more channels through which you can offer your goods the more sales you have. There are a number of companies out there who have developed software to help diversify your product so that it sells through multi-channels.

The importance of multi-channel marketing

Multi-channel marketing is important for the simple reason that you must be where your customers are. And they are everywhere. If you need another reason, consider this: Multi-channel customers spend three to four times more than single-channel customers do.

There's no doubt that customers today have much more control over the buying process than marketers do. Thanks to the proliferation of available channels, customers have more choices than ever when it comes to how they want to get information. Today there are more ways to reach customers – both in terms of number and variety of channels – than we could have imagined not so long ago. And as the number of channels continues to rise – and it will – the need to embrace multichannel marketing will become not only a good idea, but a critical one.

In addition to the above, if you have developed your e-commerce business to the point where you have your products on a number of platforms at once, and there are a lot of different sites you can advertise on, as we have seen from the previous chapter, you need a way of managing your enterprise so that you are not constantly going from one site to another to gain information on sales etc. Although you can use the tools and interfaces that each site offers, it is better to try to streamline the process. This is where multi-channel software comes in. Using the correct multi-channel partner can help streamline your ecommerce business and help you to grow further.

In the first instance, it is vital that you use a UK company as experience of the UK e-commerce industry is essential. In the second instance, you need to know exactly what it is you want from a multi-channel firm. You also need to know what marketplaces they support. For certain they will support eBay and Amazon but will they cover smaller sites?

It is well worth investigating various multi-channel firms, but make sure you know what it is that you are asking. the following are useful questions:

- What does the service cost? many firms charge a monthly subscription, some a one off payment and others a percentage of turnover-the one common denominator is that none are cheap.

- have they got what you need-what do they offer-do they offer design, accountancy, stock control and any other facilities that can help to streamline and push your operation forward.
- What is their customer service like-make sure that once they have sold you the product you get sufficient back up and customer support. I think we all have examples of companies talking the talk and disappearing when things go wrong.

The best thing for you to do is to approach various multi-channel software firms (when you are ready) and find out what exactly they can offer you to help grow your business. Below are listed a number of companies operating in the UK marketplace. None of them have been experienced by me, so I am not recommending them, just providing information.

www.channeladvisor.co.uk

ChannelAdvisor is a well established business. Well worth a look in. Fees will depend on what level of service you want.

eSellerPro www.eSellerpro.com

This firm, based in the UK, offers to integrate a retailers entire inline sales process. It has a good reputation. There is a start up fee and a monthly management fee.

Brightpearl www.brightpearl.com

Offers a comprehensive multi-channel service and charges a basic £69 a month and charges for extras such as phone service support.

ChannelGrabber www.ChannelGrabber.com

Based in the UK, ChannelGrabber supports eBay, Amazon and other sites. The basic fee for this service is £60 per month for basic packages.

Two other sites worth checking out are Storefeeder www.storefeeder.com which offers a 30 day free trial and SellerExpress at www.sellerexpress.com.

****

Chapter 13

Understanding Business Structures

Although not directly connected to selling on eBay or any other sites such as Amazon, this brief chapter will outline basic business structures which may be relevant to you if your business takes off. Regardless of how you make your money it still needs to be accounted for and HMRC will be interested, as they are in all business.

There are various structures within which your business can operate and it is essential, when formulating your business plan that you understand the nature of each structure.

The Sole or proprietary business

This is a business owned by one person. If you are operating alone then this may be suitable for your purposes. The person and the business are legally one and the same. It does not matter what or who you trade as, the business is inseparable from yourself, as opposed to a limited company, which is a separate entity. All financial risk is taken by that one person and all that persons assets are included in that risk. The one big advantage is that all decisions can be taken by the one person without interference.

A second advantage is that the administrative costs of running a sole business are small. If your business is VAT registered then you will need to keep records, as you will for Her Majesty's Revenue and Customs. However, there are no other legal requirements.

Partnerships

Partnership is a business where two or more people are joined by an agreement to run that business together. The agreement is usually written, given the potential pitfalls that can arise from a partnership. Liabilities which may arise are shared jointly and severally and this should be made clear to anyone entering a partnership. Even if you only have 1% of the business you will still be responsible for 100% of the liability. All personal assets of each partner are at risk if the business fails.

Decisions are taken jointly, as laid down by the partnership agreement. If the agreement lays down that partners have differing decision-making capacity dependent upon their shareholding then it could be that, in a three way partnership, the decision making process may be hampered because a decision cannot be reached unless the major investor is present.

It is very important indeed to consider the nature of the agreement that you are entering into and it may also be advisable to take legal advice.

Partnership usually reflects the way that business was capitalised although other factors may be taken into consideration. For example, an expert in a particular field may join with an investor to create a 50/50 partnership.

94

It is very advisable to consider carefully the ramifications of entering into a partnership. Many such arrangements end in tears, with both partners hostile to each other. Personal bankruptcy can occur as can the ruin of the partner(s). Profits are usually shared between partners in accordance with the terms in the agreement.

The Limited liability company

This type of company has evolved over the years and provides a framework within which a business can operate effectively. A limited company is usually the best vehicle for all but the smallest of businesses. It is certainly the only sensible answer if capital is being introduced by those who are not actively involved in running the business (shareholders).

Shareholders inject capital and receive a return (dividend) in proportion to the capital they invest. They are eligible to attend an annual general meeting to approve or otherwise the way the directors are running the business. Annual General meetings also determine how much of the profit will be distributed to shareholders.

Voting is in accordance with the number of shares held and the meeting can replace all or any of the directors if a majority are dissatisfied with them. Shareholders can, if a majority request, call an Extraordinary General meeting to question directors about performance, outside the Cycle of Annual General Meetings. Control of the company is in the hands of directors who are appointed by the shareholders to run the company on their behalf.

The company is a legal entity in its own right and stands alone from the directors and shareholders, who have limited liability. When a

95

company is created it will have an "Authorised Shareholding" That specifies the limit of a shareholders liability. If all shares have been issued then shareholders are not liable for any more debts that the company may accrue.

Patents and Registered designs

In order to grow, industry must continually create and develop new ideas. Innovation is expensive and innovators need protection, to ensure that others cannot pirate their ideas. All of the above items are known as "intellectual property" and, with the exception of copyright, in order to register and protect your intellectual property, if you have any associated with your eBay or Amazon business, you need to contact the patent office. Their address can be obtained from the Chartered Institute of Patent Attorneys on 0207 405 9450 www.cipa.org.uk

Patent

If you or your company have produced what you consider is a unique product or process, it is very important to register it as soon as possible, before disclosing it to anyone. The granting of a patent gives the patentee a monopoly to make, use or sell an invention for a fixed period of time. This is currently a maximum of twenty years.

Registered designs

This involves registering what you consider to be a new design. The proprietor must register before offering for sale in the U.K the new design.

Trademarks

A trademark is a means of identification-whether a word or a logo-which is used in the course of trade in order to identify and distinguish to the purchaser that the goods in question are yours. A good trademark is a very important marketing aid and you are strongly advised to register it.

Service marks

This register extends the trademark to cover not only goods but also services. If you are running a hotel for example, you can now register your service mark if you have one.

Copyright

Unlike the other four categories, copyright is established by evidence of creation, and protection is automatic. To safeguard your position, it might be sensible to deposit your work with your bank or your solicitor or send a copy of your work to yourself by registered post. It should be noted that there is no copyright attached to a name or title, only the work itself.

The above information concerning business structures and protection of goods and assets will be relevant to you, in particular when your business takes off and you cease to be an individual sitting in front of a computer selling individual items. A rudimentary knowledge of business structures is very necessary.

****

PART 2.

SETTING UP YOUR OWN BUSINESS ONLINE

Chapter 14

Setting up Your Own Business Online

Having discussed setting yourself up as a trader on eBay and Amazon, it is worthwhile briefly looking at setting up your own website, or store, independently of the big ones, and launching yourself as an online trader. Many of the lessons learnt from the previous chapters are relevant to what we will discuss below.

If you don't have the technical expertise to create your own website, and most people don't, then you will need to have a very clear idea of what it is you are trying to create and find someone to work with. You will also have to have a clear idea of what your initial budget is for your website. There are certain questions that you need to ask, such as:

- Do you know what it is that you require from your website?
- How many products will you be offering?
- What will be the ongoing maintenance requirements of the site, will you want to regularly change the appearance of the site?
- Who exactly are you trying to target with your site?

Website developers won't really be interested in your longer term business plan but will require a well worked out brief. It is essential that you look at websites selling similar content so you can get an idea of what it is you are trying to achieve. As a start you should write down the following:

- How many pages will your site require? In the first instance you don't need to worry about the pages that display products as these will be dynamically created as the site is developed. Of more importance is the number of static pages, such as 'contact us' 'about us' privacy policy and so on. When you have identified the static pages you are well on the way to creating an initial sitemap.

- Note down the content and structure of the site, what is it that your site will contain, is it just text and images or will there be downloads, video clips and review sections etc.? By identifying this you will assist the developer in deciding on the most suitable technology for the site.

- Future content management. Who will do this in the future and how often will it need to be modified?

- Marketing. You will need to have an idea of which on and offline marketing channels you plan to use in conjunction with the business, so your developer can build in the functionality at the outset to allow this to happen in the future.

- Website monitoring. You will almost certainly want to know how well your site is performing in terms of number of visitors and sales. You will also want to know where the traffic is coming from. Make allowances to integrate tools such as Google Analytics into the site. If you are planning an e-commerce store, you will want more detailed financial reporting, not only basic sales information but also tools to manage returns, stock levels, VAT and so on.

Choosing a web developer

It's true to say that there are now literally thousands of website developers around, ranging from those with very little knowledge, they may have completed a basic course, to the more technically proficient

102

and experienced. It is therefore important, given the importance of getting it right at the outset, to carry out research on a number of developers. You will want to look carefully at the areas listed below.

Experience

You will want to assess how long the developer has been operating and what their track record is, what they have developed in the past. It would be a wise move to choose a developer who has had experience of developing websites for similar companies and therefore knows the requirements. An experienced developer will be able to discuss various technology options with you and the good and bad points associated with each.

Development skills and knowledge

It is likely that the developer that you are employing will have a far greater knowledge of web technology than you. However, you can ask such questions as do they intend to build the website from scratch, or are they using an 'off the shelf' model, i.e. one that has been developed or partially developed for someone else?

If you are planning to sell products online then you will want to know their views on e-commerce/shopping basket solutions, whether they recommend PayPal or Worldpay for example (more about these later) can they set up a facility to pay by credit card and also will there be a basic content management system which will allow you or your staff to edit and delete items on the site without continuous recourse to the developer?

References from other clients

Any web developer worth his or her salt will not object to you asking other clients about the performance of the developer. As the investment in a website is one of the early major investments then it is of the utmost importance that some form of reference is taken up.

Future project management

You will want to ensure that the chosen developer explains how the process of developing the site works. You will need to ensure that it is brought in well within time and budget. Basic questions are: how often will you be informed of progress, who your contacts are and how can they be reached. In addition, you will need to ascertain how flexible the developer is if you want to add or subtract a feature to the website half way through development.

There are other aspects of development that you need to take on board, such as where the developer is based, how accessible they are, what are their education and qualifications and also, vitally, can you get on with them. You will have fairly close contact with the developer and you need to ensure that you have a good personal relationship with them. Communication is everything!

Website security and payment methods

Website security, and particularly security involving the taking of money over your site, for products and services, means having a legal responsibility to protect customer data. The worst case is someone's personal information being abstracted from your site and ending up in the hands of scammers. This has been a major headache for online business for a long time now. Although in the main, regular internet connections between the user and the web are secure, because it doesn't place the user at risk, you will need to integrate a Secure Sockets layer for protection which will give protection and provides a safe way for client and server to communicate. Essentially, SSL protocol encrypts the data being sent over the net between client and server which renders it useless to any third party. You know your connection to a website is secure when the web address begins with https:// and you might also, on some browsers notice a closed padlock icon.

The SSL can be added to the site by your developer without difficulty. Ordinarily, the vast majority of your website will be accessed in the normal way until you reach the point when the user wishes to pay for goods. It is very wise to indicate on your site that you employ SSL, which will give customers confidence to carry out their transactions and to pass on their personal payment details. Failure to indicate that the method is secure can cost you sales, simply because we are living in a time of heightened awareness of scamming.

Payment methods over the web

There are a number of ways to facilitate payment over the web. The main one with eBay and other sites will be PayPal. However, you may choose other options for your own independent store. The key point here is that the chosen method will need to be integrated by the designer. To enable online payment you will need to set up a payment gateway and a merchant account. However, as we will see, there are several ways, some simpler than others to set up a gateway. Payment gateways are an interface between your website, and the banks/card issuers around the world. There are a large number of providers and you can choose to work with a specialist provider or your own bank.

Your own bank will invariably be happy to set up this gateway with you. You will need to look at the various methods on offer and compare the fees. Some charge more than others. Most providers will charge on a scale, meaning that the more transactions the cheaper it becomes. This may not be the best deal for a start-up business, as your initial traffic and sales will be slow to build up. A merchant account is a depository into which funds you receive from online payments are made. This is one option. However, whichever option you choose, the process works as follows:

Step 1. Customer enters card details on your website.

Step 2. The card is authenticated-the details are sent via your payment gateway, to the card issuer. If the card details cannot be verified then the card will be declined.

Step 3. Payment authorization-The issuing bank checks that the cardholder's details are correct and that there are enough funds to cover the transaction and that the card hasn't been reported lost or stolen. Once all checks are carried out then an instruction is sent to the bank to debit funds.

Step 4. Payment settlement-your account is credited within a few days of the actual transaction.

Arguably the most popular payment method which can easily be integrated into your site is PayPal. It provides a simple method for payment and the costs are low, particularly for a new business. There are other payment methods similar to PayPal which can be explored on the web.

The process of ordering

We will be discussing the creation of content on your site in the chapter on marketing, however, at this stage it is essential to ensure that once customers have chosen a product or service then they can actually complete the ordering process, and that it is an easy path. I know from my own experience that a process that is too long-winded can work against the business and can lose you sales.

Ensure that the A-Z process is simple

Part of an integrated system for purchasing over a website is what is known as the 'shopping basket'. I am sure that you will have seen this on Amazon or similar sites. You are invited to place items in a shopping trolley before checkout. This gives the feeling that you are in an actual store. This is known as the order pipeline and is the process and the number of pages that a consumer must navigate before the completion of the sale. It is important that the order pipeline has as few stages as possible so that the customer doesn't become frustrated. Therefore, you need to define what details are essential to complete the order and what information can be captured at a later date.

* * * * * * * * * * * * * *

Chapter 15

Exploiting Your Sites Potential

Making additional Money from Your Site

Once you have set your website up, you can start thinking about making money from day one. You can earn money from activities quite apart from your mainstream business.

One of the main areas for generating extra revenue is that of advertising. Choosing to display advertising on your website is a good way to earn extra money. Basically, users of your site will see advertising and if they like what they see then they will click on the advert. This is what generates the money, each click earns you money, the amount varying with the advertiser. However, for this to work you must have enough traffic on your site to bring in potential 'clickers'

The problem with advertising is that it can serve to cheapen a site. Typically, people go over the top when setting up banner adverts on their site and the end result is that there are scores of adverts selling products which have little or nothing to do with the core product that you sell. This will serve as a distraction and people will rapidly leave your site.

For example, your business might be publishing and related industries. To have your website plastered with ads for car insurance and holidays in the sun would be counterproductive. However, to advertise the consumer magazine 'Which' would be a far better fit. Therefore, you need to give a lot of thought to what adverts you want on your site, if you want to maintain the integrity of your site.

Signing up with Google Adsense is relatively simple as is the integration into your site. You can use Google's back office tools to select the type of advertising that you want.

Display, or banner ads usually use the CPC (cost per click) or CPM (cost per thousand) model. Basically, you get paid for every click or every thousand clicks.

You need to keep grounded about the potential money you might earn from this, as the big earners are of course Google, Facebook and the like. Also, take a look at your own behaviour. When you surf the web, alight on sites, how many times do you actually click on adverts.

The main advice to you is that when deciding to place adverts on your site, don't go mad in the hope of earning money, as this can ruin your site, cheapen it and confuse the user. Also, the dreamed of riches from placing ads can be pie in the sky! Concentrate on your core business, selling your product or service to the public and treat any revenues from advertising as a secondary minor source of revenue.

Selling third party products

In addition to advertising, the web offers a wide variety of potential revenue streams. Even if your business sells specialist products and you would rather not plaster your site with advertising there are a number of digital products that you can promote on your site. For example, organizations such as CLICKBANK www.clickbank.com have many thousands of products that you can promote.

The following are some of the features:

- Commissions are on a sliding scale, some offering up to 75% per sale
- There is an opportunity to earn ongoing revenue from subscription based products
- You can obtain full back-office statistics to help you manage the process.

You should visit their website, outlined above, for more information. This may or may not be for you but it is another opportunity to maximise revenue.

Affiliation

Affiliation is easy to implement both as an advertiser (those who want others to help them sell their product or service and pay a commission) or alternatively as a publisher where you help sell the goods and services of others and earn a commission. It can be, although again be realistic, a very good way of generating revenue online without too much involvement. Basically, you are a conduit for traffic for your chosen affiliate/partner and you make money earning a commission every time one of your visitors clicks on a link or interacts with your advertiser's site through your site.

Many people might choose to work with a large organisation such as Amazon, become an Amazon Associate, If you don't want to work with a single provider, or you don't want to promote the products that a particular organisation sells then you can investigate Affiliation Networks.

Affiliate Networks

Affiliate networks are big business. They match advertisers with publishers (companies selling with those who will promote goods). Affiliate networks vary in size, reputation and ability to attract highest profile advertisers and publishers. The more successful networks will charge advertisers a fee to join the programme and more often than not a monthly fee for managing the account. It is usually free to become a publisher and that's why it can prove a lucrative earner for your site. Affiliate networks make their money from the set up and monthly fees paid by advertisers along with a commission of the total revenue generated for the client.

Product feeds

Accepting a product feed from an advertiser can require some development work but what this gives you is the ability to display as many or as few products as you wish to from an advertisers website. For example, if your business is that of publishing you can promote books and magazines, with product names, descriptions and pricing etc. What you are essentially doing is to promote someone else's products straight from their site. Product feeds are a very effective way to build up a large website quickly. It is an effective way to sell a product online without the risk. www.productfeed.org is a useful website to visit.

****

Chapter 16

Supplying Goods and Services-The Supply Chain

Setting up your business and supplying goods and services

As with operating as an eBay seller, one of the most important elements of any business is making sure that it can provide goods, good quality goods, on time. We will be talking about the final link in the business chain a little later, good customer service. This chapter is about sourcing and supplying the actual goods. The goods that you supply will be totally dependent on the type of business that you are running, whether you are selling actual physical goods or digital goods for example.

Local suppliers

If you are selling physical goods, if you can find a local supplier this will be a great advantage. The closer to home the supplier then the greater control that you will have. Local can mean anywhere within the UK. Local products mean reduced costs, lower freight charges, free local delivery or self-service pick up options. This will all help to save money. Also, local suppliers mean better stock management in that local suppliers can often hold onto stock until consignment.

Buying from abroad

Many products can be sourced cheaply from abroad, particularly from places such as China. Buying products from countries such as these will no doubt help to improve your profitability in the long run. However, unless you have the time to go to the relevant country and purchase goods, and you are fully aware of the tax implications, then all sorts of risks are presented.

Even if you cannot find the time or money to visit a potential trading partner abroad, there are many online trading platforms offering a huge range of potential suppliers and goods, (Business-to-Business platforms). Many charge businesses to advertise their contact details and place descriptions of their products, others will charge buyers a membership fee to gain access to contact details, some others charge a commission. A few such trading platforms are:

- www.alibaba.com
- www.tradekey.com
- www.globalsources.com
- www.diytrade.com

There are many more. Eventually you will want to meet suppliers and forge a relationship. There is nothing better than this to ensure confidence and security and to discuss trade terms.

Choosing a supplier of goods

You should keep all the data that you receive from the various potential suppliers. The name of the game is competition. For instance, when you have set up your business and are ready to go, you might eventually run into problems with your suppliers for a variety of reasons, price, service delivery, customer care and so on, and may want to switch supplier. You should build up a data bank of suppliers so that you are in a position to move if necessary.

Managing the suppliers

Maintaining good relations with your suppliers is as important as managing your customers. Suppliers are very important, without them you don't really have a business. Managing suppliers well is wholly dependent on how well you communicate with them. There are many instances of relationships starting off well and then something goes wrong and the whole pack of cards collapses.

The essence of good management is face-to-face communication. Find time to meet on a regular basis with your suppliers. Remember they have their own pressures too, so sit down and talk about any problems that may arise. That goes a long way.

Organising payment terms

With a new business, it is highly unlikely that you will be given immediate credit by suppliers. Even if you are known personally to the supplier from a previous life, the first order will have to be paid up front.

However, once you have a history with a supplier, once you have maintained regular payments, then it is likely that you will be given time to pay. Usually, 30 days from invoice date is the norm. The same goes with your business bank account. In the first instance it is very unlikely that you will be given generous business overdraft terms. Again, it will be dependent on your track record. our relationship with a supplier begins from the word go, when you place your first order. Make sure that the account information that they have is correct, the billing address, delivery address, contact

115

numbers and email address, along with VAT number if applicable and payment terms.

When you receive an order be rigorous and check that the contents are what you ordered and that the quantity is correct. Mistakes can happen and they should be rectified at the outset otherwise problems can arise.

Breaking off relationships with a supplier

No matter how good the relationship is with your supplier, there may come a time when you will need to sever ties. It may be that things started to go wrong and they have progressively got worse. There could have been a change of personnel and the time and effort that has been expended building up a relationship has all gone out of the window. Whatever, it is time to switch.

Once you have found a replacement supplier then you will need to notify your existing supplier that you no longer require their services and that all outstanding invoices will be paid. Although feelings may have been hurt, business comes first. It is highly likely that you will have warned your supplier beforehand of problems so it may not come as a shock.

Stock control

The type of business that you run and the type of goods that you provide, will determine the level of stock control that will be required. If someone is ordering from you and you order the goods from someone else and they are delivered direct to the buyer's door then the whole process of stock control is simple. However, if you are buying goods in bulk at one price and delivering direct to the customer yourself then this will require a different system. To run your e-commerce store smoothly from the outset, you will need to make sure that you have the correct tools to do this.

Bar code printer

Depending on the type of products that you are planning to sell and how far up the supply chain you are sourcing your products, you will need to obtain a bar code printer. Bar codes make light work of stock management and a bar code printer will prove invaluable if you need to label your product.

Bar code scanners

To assist you in both receiving and picking and packing customer orders, a barcode scanner will be most useful. Setting up your back office will take time initially as you assign each and every product a bar code but once done then stock can move quickly into and out of the warehouse.

Stock management systems

In the first instance, a simple spreadsheet might suffice to keep accurate records of stock movement. However, as your business grows and becomes more complex it is likely that you will need a more sophisticated system. There are a number of systems around that might be suitable and if you require a demonstration it is likely that a company would be willing to do this for you.

Invoicing customers

Controlling cash flow is the lifeblood of any business. Spending money is easy but getting the money in can be a different story. It is your legal obligation to provide customers with an invoice and a receipt along with every order shipped. Invoices can detail numerous orders on one sheet. The invoice must contain basic details, such as your company address and your registration details plus VAT number if applicable. The customer's order must be fully outlined and also the price that they have paid. Whilst all of this

117

sounds obvious it is amazing how many companies send out inadequate invoices which are then not paid. In addition, it goes without saying that invoices must be tracked and late payers contacted immediately. Strong credit control is vitally important. Again, it is amazing how many companies send out invoices then lose track of them doing nothing about them until they accidentally discover, or their accountant discovers, that they haven't been paid.

The storage of stock

If you are in a position where you have to store stock before delivery then there are a few basic rules that you should observe:

- Make sure that where you store your stock is appropriate-i.e. it is dry and clean and suits the goods that you plan to store. Any damage to goods once delivered from the original supplier to you will be down to you
- Make sure that the storage is secure and protected from fire or theft-ensure adequate alarms and also current insurance is in place
- Make sure that you have adequate systems in place to check goods received. If the incorrect number of goods arrives, or there is damage this should be dealt with then and there
- Carry out regular stock takes. This becomes more important as the business grows.
- Make sure that stock is stored in a logical and ordered way. Have clearly numbered areas where specific stock resides so it can be found easily

Picking and packing stock

In the first instance, the picking of stock may not be a great problem as your business will probably be small. However, it is

118

when it grows that it can become more complex.
The following are tips for you when organising the selection of stock:

- You should have a picking list which enables you to go straight to the item you want. This will save time and effort
- Ensure that an invoice/receipt is sent with every order
- If you don't have all the items when packing the order notify the customer straight away
- Ensure items are well packaged to avoid damage

Delivery of items

This is always a contentious area. My own experience of delivery has been that, no matter how much companies put into promoting the product and making all sorts of promises, the end link in the chain, delivery of items, lets them down. There is nothing worse than a surly delivery driver virtually throwing the goods at you or refusing to carry goods up the stairs or whatever. In short, rudeness and inflexibility. I hasten to add that this isn't true across the board but it is in many cases. Given that everything about online shopping should be about convenience, including delivery, then it is important to choose the right partner, which could be Royal Mail, FedEx or any one of the delivery companies. Usually, you would sign a deal with one or other that can guarantee price and also provide some sort of track record when it comes to delivery.

Courier companies will usually offer attractive rates for volume deliveries so it will be up to you to negotiate the appropriate contract. You should look for the following:

- Courier companies who will collect from your address and can give specified times for delivery
- Some companies will also handle returns as part of the

119

contract, make sure that this is in your contract

- International orders are slightly different-they must have a customs statement from your company clearly marked on the outside of the package which includes a description of the contents. You can check with www.hmrc.gov.uk for more information.

Returns

There are a number of reasons why returns are made: incorrect goods sent to the customer, damaged goods or customer changes his or her mind. Whatever the reason, returns happen and have to be dealt with. The following are useful tips when dealing with returns:

- When the good is returned check the damage, if damage is alleged, to see whether this is down to you or to the manufacturer
- Make sure you keep an accurate record of returns and adjust stock accordingly
- Acknowledge that you have received the return-this is good customer service and might encourage the customer to buy again
- Keep an eye of people who buy and return on a regular basis-this can happen, especially with items such as DVD's, which can be copied. After a while you can sort out those who are operating this kind of scam.

****

Chapter 17

Internet Marketing

Each business has its own overall budget and also goals and targets. In the ideal world it would be nice to be able to invest in both offline and online marketing. However, the reality for most businesses, particularly start-ups, is that funds are limited. In this case, it is crucial to understand the techniques used in online marketing.

Search engine optimization

Most users of the internet will begin the buying process with a search engine. Search engines are enormously powerful and therefore it is essential that your website is built, maintained and updated to be both customer and search engine friendly. Effective search engine optimization is about making your website visible to the search engines, primarily Google.

Making your site visible to search engines

Your site has to be seen to be ranked. Google uses software called Googlebot to scan individual web pages on the internet and what it finds has a direct impact on how thoroughly your site is indexed and how it can rank in the natural Search Engine Results Pages (SERPS).

Quality content

Good content is the key to a good website. Good content will sell your product. Good content will mean that more and more users will visit your site and become consumers of your products and services. In addition, if you have good content then other websites will want to link up to your site therefore increasing the flow of traffic. If your site and its content is seen as good by Google then it will be ranked higher. People looking for a specific good or service will go straight to your site, bypassing the competition. However, in order to ensure that this is the case, your site should be well designed and regularly maintained and updated.

A by-product of creating good content on your website is that other websites will want to link to your content. This can only be good because it puts your website in a position of being an authority on your given product or service. It will result in more traffic to your site and will attract the attention of Google, improving your rankings. It is no good developing a site which looks attractive and then not maintaining it or trying to optimize your rankings. This will set you back and if you are relying more on people finding your site, as opposed to the more traditional forms of marketing, then it is essential to have an ongoing plan for updating and promoting your site.

The use of Key words and phrases

You will want to find your main, or niche, keywords and concentrate on writing content to exploit the words. Keywords are the tool through which those who search the web find your unique product. If you are selling bathrooms for example you will want to come up with as many associated words as possible such as 'designer bathrooms' or 'Victorian bathrooms' in other words try to differentiate and provide as many entries as possible for the user. To just use the word 'bathroom' will severely limit the access to your own site.

Search engine marketing

SEM, Paid Search or PPC advertising is a broad subject that will require research on your part to ensure that you know what you are doing before you invest heavily.

SEM allows you to display an advert on the Search Engine Results Pages or the Search Engines network of publisher websites which you can target to display only to users searching for specific keywords or phrases related to your business. You control your account totally, from the text or images of the advert to how much you wish to spend.

If you elect to run PPC adverts with Google, then your ads will be displayed above and to the right of the organic or natural search results, i.e. the sponsored area. Google calls its program Adwords, which is where the search engine makes most of its profits. There are a number of reasons why search engine marketing is effective:

- It is quick to get started
- You are in control of what you spend
- Your campaigns give you instant visibility

What Google has done with Adwords is to create an online auction for every keyword and phrase in every language. The more competitive a keyword, the higher the price. This is how Google makes its money.

You should start your Adwords campaign with a small budget, dip your toe in the water, to see how you go. Setting up an account is simple enough and you should ensure that you read the help and FAQ's on the site before committing yourself.

Adwords works by charging you a fee every time someone clicks on your advert-the more you are willing to pay in comparison to others bidding for the same keywords and the better your landing page is (Quality Score) the higher up the sponsored links you will be placed. The bigger your budget, the more users will be shown your advert and the more that will click through. As soon as your budget has been spent, your advert is taken off until the next day. This allows you to keep tight control of your marketing spend and allows you to see very quickly if the campaign is working and to measure the return on your investment.

Purchasing traffic

When you enter into Google Adwords or place a banner ad on another website you are in effect buying traffic to your site. There are some unscrupulous companies around that charge you for delivering visitors to your site and then don't deliver.

Legitimate performance marketing companies do exist and they are well aware of the business need for traffic. They are also quite sophisticated and can direct the right sort of traffic to your site. Performance marketing companies invest heavily in building up their own network of users or publisher's websites which they then exploit by showing their advertiser's (your) sales message to their network. By carefully categorizing and segmenting their user base, they can effectively ensure that your pages are shown to relevant users. If someone wants law books for example they will only show your advertisement to those interested in law books.

Depending on the size and nature of the performance marketing company you can specify the countries in which you want your advert to be shown or even the approximate age or gender of the target audience. The more specific your requirements the more you will be charged for the service. However, because it is performance based, you will only pay when the campaign results in a conversion.

The following are a sample of companies that offer Performance marketing.

Burst www.burstmedia.com

DoubleClick www.doubleclick.com

ValueClick Media www.conversantmedia.com

There are many more!

Email marketing

Email marketing is an effective way to send your message before you have had a chance of building up your own database of customers. Performance marketing companies will provide lists that are segmented by interest. You will need to check with the provider that all addresses have been cleared and have given their consent to receive third party promotional emails. I receive many such emails every day which I have not consented to and which I delete, so it is important to do your homework beforehand.

Affiliation (as advertiser)

There are a wide variety of affiliation networks available which marry advertisers to publishers. Most networks charge new advertisers a set-up fee which gives your business access to the network of affiliates. Set-up fees can be hefty so you need to go into this with care. In addition, most networks charge advertisers a monthly fee which covers continued access to the network. Ongoing performance can be monitored through the networks portal and affiliates reports can be generated. The strongest aspect of affiliation is payment on performance. You only pay a commission if your affiliate delivers a lead, registration or sale. You are free to pay as much or as little as you want for each of these conversions. Affiliates take campaigns seriously and invest time, money and effort to promote advertiser's products and services. The relationship is two way and you also have to be serious, keeping them up to date with new products, pricing and any offers or promotions that you intend to run. As with all aspects of business, good communication is the key.

Using vouchers and coupons

The use of vouchers and coupons to promote and sell products, usually at a discount, is becoming increasingly popular with online business. The idea has been around for ever, being used for all sorts of off-line business but it is now being used for online trading.

Coupons usually allow customers, whether existing or new, to benefit from a promotion by entering a code online at the point of purchasing. The utilization of the code will modify the customers order in some way corresponding to the offer.

These coupons can be printed and distributed through print media, handed out in the street as a flyer or as part of promotional literature, or through any other medium. they can also be distributed online by adding the coupon to a social media post such as facebook or twitter. They can also be sent to existing customers in a mailshot.

The use of coupons as part of your selling strategy will require some work to your site and again this is what you will be asking your web designer to do for you.

Co-registration

Co-registration is a lead and customer acquisition strategy used by numerous brands. It is performance based-you only pay on results. Co-registration involves placing a short text or image advertisement for your company on the registration pages of high volume third party websites or landing pages. Usually, you are sharing the page with other advertisers who sell similar products or services, or the page is themed in such a way as to link the advertisers. This method of promotion allows users to request additional information about your product or service and in turn provides you with their contact details.

Co-registration allows you to build a permission based, targeted database of consumers interested in your service and, depending on the volume of the third party site, allows you to develop lists very quickly.

Rich media

Rich media is, basically, videos, pod casts and other images which will serve to improve your visibility and differentiate you from other sites selling similar products. Most shop windows have excellent displays and lure customers in. Web portals should be the same and a short video can do wonders when it comes to displaying your product, or telling customers more about you and your company and what products or services you sell.

Social media

Social media, such as Facebook and Twitter is now so widespread that it would be foolish not to advertise your existence on their sites. By opening accounts with platforms such as Facebook, Twitter and Linked In you will be able to reach your potential audience and also hear what is being said about your company, product or service.

Blogging

Adding a blog to your business website is a simple procedure for any web developer and the quality and customization options from the big payers such as Wordspace and Blogger leaves very little need to develop your own platform. A blog will allow you to produce articles, presenting news and comment about your business and its operations. Blogging helps to develop brand building and may provide you with competitive advantage..

Market places

Market places such as Ebay can be very useful. Although initially conceived as a site where individuals can buy and sell, it now has a facility for professional sellers. Ebay and Amazon in the UK, and Priceminister and Play in Europe, among a few others, provide online business the opportunity to enjoy a worldwide audience by listing your products or services and offering them to their enormous customer base. By paying a listing fee, or a monthly fee plus a share or percentage of the sale price, your business can gain enormous reach within a very short time.

To make it easy for businesses to sell via marketplace sites, these online sellers offer a route to professional sellers to be able to bulk load their products. This is achieved through XML, CSV or through an online portal. There will be some work involved on your side adapting your product database to the platforms particular product classification rules, but once that is done, it is usually a straightforward process loading your products.

The listing fee, commission on sale and other fees can tend to be high if you are selling low margin items. However, the sheer size of the audience can make it worthwhile. As with many other things, it is a case of trying it, dipping your toe in the water and see whether it is worth carrying on.

****

Chapter 18

Keeping the Customer Happy

Customer Service

If you have set yourself up as an eBay trader or trader on Amazon you will receive feedback which will affect the perception of your site. If you are operating as a trader independent of the big sites then you will need to keep your eye on the customer services ball.

With any business, managing customer relationships is vitally important. When they have purchased a good, or goods or services, the customer likes to feel valued and treated well. If they do, they themselves will come back to your site and will recommend your business to others.

Your business will have a policy which will promise a level of service delivery. You might promise next day delivery, you might offer a free gift with goods and services. Make sure that you run your business in line with your policy. Don't get sloppy. Remember that you will be up against competition. The way for you to keep customers and develop your customer base is for you to keep them satisfied. It doesn't take long for word to get about that your business fails to deliver.

Make sure that people can access your site

This may sound obvious. If people cannot access your site for some reason then you haven't got a business. There are now a proliferation of devices that can access the internet, from mobile phones to tablet devices. In addition to the range of devices around, you need to consider the whole range of potential users in order to ensure that no one is left out of the frame and that all possible customers can access the site and see your products. This includes disabled, blind, deaf and older web users. Your web designer will, or should, know the ways to ensure that your site is laid out to ensure maximum accessibility.

The relationship with a customer begins from them becoming aware of your business and website, and then from the first click which gives them access to your site. Your homepage has to be clear and uncluttered and also needs to be clear and straightforward enabling the potential customer to see the product and go through to the ordering page and buy. We have talked about advertising on your site to gain extra revenues. Be careful that you don't plaster the site with inappropriate ads that serve to confuse and annoy the customer and ultimately drive them away.

Another very important aspect of your business is the ease of communication with your company. For example, I use Google and am a member of their partner programme and, in the past, they have been absolutely impossible to contact. They used to have a support line but that is now gone and they could not be contacted personally. I ended up writing to their headquarters in California with my grievance. This experience fostered within me the feeling that I no longer wished to deal with them. They became faceless and anonymous. To be fair, I think that they received enough complaints to focus their minds son improving the problem. Make very sure that this is not the case with your business. Ensure that there is an address and telephone number as well as an email so that customers can phone you up. This is most important. It is also useful to have a frequently asked questions page so that people can find answers without contacting you personally.

Terms and conditions

An online business will have, or should have, a terms and conditions page. Most users, when they purchase something, will click the little box to state that they have read and understood the terms and conditions of that business and what it offers. The reality is that most people don't read them as it is boring. However, as a business owner, the terms and conditions of the business are crucial. Your terms and conditions will outline exactly what is expected of users of the site and what users can expect from the business. You might want to take a look at the terms and conditions of another business and also take legal advice before you formulate yours. It is very important to have a privacy policy which is, essentially, a document which outlines your policy in respect of what customer information you will collect, and what you plan to do with this information now and in the future.

Customers can be suspicious especially now with the rise of online identity theft and they will need reassurance. When you create your privacy policy you will need to be very clear about what you intend to do with customer's information. In all likelihood this will be retained for your own use and you won't be doing anything with it. Having thought this through then you should make sure that this is enshrined in a privacy policy and put up onto your site. This will go a long way to reassuring customers.

Customer service

There is a lot to customer service, over and above offering a phone number and address on the website. You will need to manage the customers who phone you up. Online business, as with all business, will have a fairly significant rate of calls from customers wanting to know where the order is, reporting damage or some aspect of the service that has either gone wrong or that they want to chase up.

Your tone with customers must, at all times and without fail, be polite and courteous and helpful, providing answers to problems. You can get some pretty rude people contacting you and it is important that you are polite but firm and answer queries tactfully. Treating customers well leads to repeat business and also recommendations to others. Before you know it your business becomes well known through word of mouth.

Customer service policies of most business will contain guidelines for the customer to follow, offering 'service promises'. Your customer service policy may typically contain the following:

- Contact details for the customer-this will typically be a phone number and e mail address plus business address.
- A guide to when customers can receive a reply-i.e. within 24 hours of contacting you.
- A promise to remedy problems as soon as possible.
- A promise of compensation if the problem is not solved in a reasonable time.

All of the above, simple though it may be, will give customers confidence in your business.

Newsletters

You might want to put together a regular newsletter talking about your business, any changes and also what's new in terms of products. You will have a list of customers to whom you can send this out and may also have obtained a mailing list from elsewhere. This newsletter will be physically sent out as opposed to emailed out.

It is important that customers opt in to receive newsletters and this can be ascertained when they first enter your site or buy a product.

Marketing by email

If you manage an email marketing campaign correctly, this can be a powerful tool in the whole marketing spectrum. As we have seen from the previous chapter traditional marketing techniques are powerful, always have been. However, with the advent of online business, email marketing can be equally powerful.

One big problem with email marketing, and I think that we all know this from experience, is that emails can be treated as just more junk, more spam to be deleted. Indeed, given the content of most email marketing, it is no surprise. Watches from Switzerland, Viagra from India, you name it. There is one common denominator here: no one touches them with a barge pole.

The first thing that you need to consider is, 'what email addresses can you use? Unless people opt in to specifically receive your e mail shots then you cannot use their address. This is because data protection laws apply to the internet. We all know that this doesn't stop legions of people sending us spam emails. However, in order to stay on the right side of the law, and to maintain the integrity of your business, you need to respect people's right to privacy. Again, on your site you will have a tick box which gives people the choice to opt in or out.

When sending out emails you need to selectively target the recipients. You will need to ensure that those who receive your emails will be interested in buying your products. This means that of all the people or business on your list, you will need to break

135

them down into clusters to identify the ones that you want to contact at any given time and with which product or service.

Content of the email

This is most important and should reflect the overall tone and content of your business. With email marketing, you need to get the message across quickly and effectively.

You will need to ensure that:

- The specific product, promotion or service is highlighted at the outset
- How the user will benefit from this product or service
- What you expect the reader of the email to do next.

You will need to design the email content to reflect the product, service or promotion. You will also have to take time and care to ensure that the benefit to the user is highlighted clearly. The benefit could be simply price or a whole host of other benefits such as legal updates, free offers to festivals and so on. Be clear and you will catch the potential customer's eye.

Finally, make sure that it is easy for the customers to move to the next step. If they need to click on a link make this obvious and provide the link. If you require a from completed keep questions to a minimum so as not to bore the person involved.

Testing your own service-Mystery shopping

Having designed your site and spent a lot of time, effort and money putting all of the aspects together you might occasionally want to test it all yourself to see if it stands up to scrutiny and to see if your business is delivering what it says. You can do this through the medium of mystery shopping.

Mystery shopping is usually associated with big business, which will send someone to one of their branches, for example, and become a customer and report back on the whole experience. Assuming that this book is being read by the smaller business person, then it might not seem so relevant.

However, you can still employ someone who is either an additional staff member or someone from outside, to go through the whole experience and come back to you with any criticisms. This person will start by clicking onto your site, reading the content, ordering, reading the privacy policy and your customer service policy, opting in for further information, ordering a good, contacting you with a query and contacting you with post-delivery feedback.

This will prove invaluable to you in ironing out any problems or perceived problems with your business. As your business grows bigger then it will become easier to employ a mystery shopper without the knowledge of staff making the experience more plausible.

****

Conclusion

I hope that you have learnt something about the process of becoming an eBay and Amazon seller, and also become aware that eBay and Amazon are only two of many. Sometimes it is well worth trying alternatives to monopolies or indeed using all the sites at your disposal to create a healthy living for yourself.

As with all retail, whether online or offline, it is all about presentation and price plus speed of delivery and good customer service, not to mention good after-sales service. It takes a while to build up a reputation as a good and trustworthy online seller and that is what you should do right at the outset.

Take time to learn and understand the sites, See what your competition is doing and how they sell, and then start off on the right foot. Your shop front has to be clear and concise and your execution of sales and delivery must be right. In this way you will become a successful seller and create a reputation for yourself.

Part two of this book dealt with creating your own online business. You can do this in conjunction with selling goods on the other sites. Many of the same principles apply. The most successful retailers out there have created a brand out of their business names. This is what you want to do, don't let it become soiled by sloppy practices.

Good luck with your venture and remember, *maintain the highest standards and treat the customer with respect.*

Index